THE BIRTH OF
Virginia's
Aristocracy

James C. Thompson II (signature)

08-20-10

James C. Thompson II

COMMONWEALTH BOOKS
Alexandria, Virginia

Commonwealth Books
1800 Edgehill Center
Alexandria, VA 22307
703-407-3719
www.commonwealthbooks.org

Library of Congress Control Number: 2009912409 (paperback edition)
ISBN (print):   978-0-9825922-0-5
ISBN (ebook): 978-0-9825922-1-2

Edited by Deb Strubel
Index by Kathleen Strattan
Cover and text design and compositon by John Reinhardt Book Design

975.2
THO
12-20-2010

Cover and title page illustration: The First Virginia Assembly, 1619

Printed in the United States of America

Acknowledgments

I HAVE BEEN ABLE to complete this work with the generous help of many people. I would like to recognize the following individuals for their contributions to its success.

First, I wish to thank the International Center for Jefferson Studies for providing me with the means for doing the research underlying the finished text. I am grateful for the opportunity to work at the Center and appreciate the kindnesses it extended to me during my tenure there.

I would also like to thank the Center's staff for making my stay comfortable and productive. In particular, I would like to thank Jack Robertson for acquiring texts that helped me in my research and Anna Burkes whose cheerful assistance made the library seem like a second home. I would also like to remember Prof. Douglas Bradburn for his insights and for his congenial company.

I would like to thank Rocque Kramer and Frank Pritchett for their support and encouragement. Completing this work would not have been possible without their help.

I would like to thank John Marshall, Steve Hopson, Bill Old and Andrew Baird for reading drafts of the book and for their comments and suggestions.

I would like to thank Deb Strubel for her skillful assistance in editing and correcting the text and John Reinhardt for transforming it into a beautiful book.

I would like to thank the members of my family for their patience and forbearance during what I am sure seemed like an endless process in formulating the text.

I would like to thank Professor Warren Billings for reading the manuscript and for helping me appreciate the difference between an academic history of Virginia's "governing class" and a philosopher's commentary on societal development in Virginia.

Finally I would like to thank Lydia Coleman for her encouragement, comments and countless other contributions to this project. I could not have not have done it without her.

I would like to add here that my training is in Philosophy not in History. When asked what the value of Philosophy is, Rene Descartes once replied that "it teaches us to speak with the appearance of knowledge on all subjects." I do not know whether Descartes counted History among this host, but I do know that that historians tend to be rather cool about History that has been passed through a philosophical filter. With this in mind, I am presenting *The Birth of Virginia's Aristocracy* as a work in the History of Ideas. Any failings in respect to the intellectual foundation upon which it rests and the information it contains are my own. Its failings, like its strengths, will be easier to evaluate as more of the titles in its series are released.

Contents

List of Illustrations

Artist unknown. Present location unknown. Used by permission of the Independence Hall Association in Philadelphia, PA on whose website, USHistory.org, the thumbnail image appearing in this book can be found.

IMAGE REFERENCE: http://images.google.com/imgres?imgurl=http://www.ushistory.org/us/images/00034315.jpg&imgrefurl=http://www.ushistory.org/us/2f.asp&usg=__eDgwIBzNbjJjA_4HBTPptyAPAWw=&h=175&w=250&sz=9&hl=en&start=3&sig2=hDVeqifjFVhl9jKKi8oDYg&um=1&tbnid=olkadFTt-i0X7M:&tbnh=78&tbnw=111&prev=/images%3Fq%3Dhouse%2Bof%2Bburgesses%2B1619%26hl%3Den%26rls%3Dcom.microsoft:en-us:IE-SearchBox%26sa%3DX%26um%3D1&ei=1P3QSsfgJNHIlAeS6eipCg

Artist unknown. Current owner and location are unknown. The thumbnail image appearing in this book is in the public domain. Efforts to contact Northbourne Sources, on whose website the thumbnail image appearing in this book can be found, failed.

IMAGE REFERENCE: http://freespace.virgin.net/andrew.parkinson4/san_intr.html.

Illustration by T. H. Robinson for The Story of Sir Walter Raleigh, Margaret Duncan Kelley, E. P. Dutton & Co, 1906. The thumbnail image appearing in this book is used with permission from Heritage-History.com

IMAGE REFERENCE: http://www.heritage-history.com/www/heritage.php?Dir=books&MenuItem=display&author=kelly&book=raleigh&story=_front

Painting by Deryck Foster (1985). The painting in presently owned by the Bank of Bermuda and is used with its permission.

IMAGE REFERENCE: http://bermuda-online.org/somersfleet.gif

List of Illustrations

List of Illustrations

Attributed to Sir Peter Lely, circa 1644. Presently in a private collection.
The thumbnail image appearing in this book is in the public domain.

IMAGE REFERENCES: http://images.google.com/imgres?imgurl=http://
www.s9.com/images/portraits/2551_Berkeley-William-Sir.
jpg&imgrefurl=http://www.s9.com/Biography/Berkeley-William-
Sir&usg=__E3MBld-L2mpybhR6YBe48QhSDSA=&h=253&w=194&sz=
8&hl=en&start=35&sig2=pCVZDFCxWPqIsvQ0-gwDkg&um=1&itbs
=1&tbnid=SDGH8duuoja3WM:&tbnh=111&tbnw=85&prev=/images%
3Fq%3DWilliam%2BBerkeley%2Bpictures%26ndsp%3D18%26hl%3Den
%26rls%3Dcom.microsoft:en-us:IE-SearchBox%26sa%3DN%26start%3
D18%26um%3D1&ei=WYAMS6_nH4OUtgOu_YmiAw.

Frontispiece for *Our Island Story*, H. E. Marshall (1920). Illustration by
Archibald Stevenson Forrest. The thumbnail image appearing in this
book is used with permission of Heritage-History.com.

IMAGE REFERENCE: www.heritage-history.com/books/marshall/isalnd/front/2.gif

Painted by Howard Pyle for "In Washington's Day" by Woodrow Wilson,
pub. in Harper's Magazine, 1896 (litho). The thumbnail image appearing
in this book is reproduced under an affiliation agreement with Allposters.
com.

THE IMAGE CAN BE PURCHASED AT: http://www.allposters.com/-sp/Sir-Wil-
liam-Berkeley-Surrendering-to-the-Commissioners-of-the-Common-
wealth-Posters_i1732139_.htm

Painting by Pieter van der Faes. The thumbnail image appearing in this
book is in the public domain.

IMAGE REFERENCE: http://www.generalmonck.com/biography.htm

Painting by Charles M. Padday depicts King Charles II arriving at Dover
in 1659. Current owner unknown. The thumbnail image appearing in
this book is reproduced under an affiliation agreement with art.com.

IMAGE CAN BE PURCHASED AT: http://www.art.com/products/p12369897-sa-
i1738805/charles-m-padday-the-restoration-charles-ii-lands-at-dover.htm

Painted by Henry Gascars during his residence in England from 1672–
1678. This image is in the public domain.

IMAGE REFERENCE: http://commons.wikimedia.org/wiki/File:James_Stu-
art,_Duke_of_York.jpg

Artist Thure Thulstrup. Current owner Virginia Historical Society. The thumbnail image reproduced in this book is with the permission of the Virginia Historical Society.

IMAGE REFERENCE: http://www.vahistorical.org/ov/meet.htm

Painted by Howard Pyle. Illustration from 'At Home in Virginia' by Woodrow Wilson, pub. in Harper's Magazine, 1896 (litho). Current Owner: Private Collection. The thumbnail image reproduced in this book is reproduced with permission from The Bridgeman Art Library.

IMAGE REFERENCE: http://www.bridgemanart.com/image/Pyle-Howard-1853-1911-after/In-the-Old-Raleigh-Tavern-illustration-from-At-Home-in-Virginia-by-Woodrow-Wilson-pub-in-Harper-s-M/b61091e5388f4e7d9f08006b3de86931?key=Howard Pyle&filter=CBIHV&thumb=x150&num=15&page=24

Painted by Howard Pyle. Oil on canvas. From "The Story of the Revolution" by Henry Cabot Lodge, published in Scribner's Magazine (March 1898). Delaware Art Museum, Wilmington, USA/Howard Pyle. The thumbnail image reproduced in this book is in the public domain.

IMAGE REFERENCE: Bridgeman Art Library, http://www.bridgemanart.com/image/Pyle-Howard-1853-1911/Thomas-Jefferson-Writing-the-Declaration-of-Independence-from-The-Story-of-the-Revolution-by-Henry-/bbe1c7d8d93a4ee1ac80e055d93dc3de?key=Howard Pyle&filter=CBPOIHV&thumb=x150&num=15&page=326

Sir Edwin Sandys (1561–1629)

Sandys was educated at Oxford. He was knighted by James I in 1603. He was an original "adventurer" in the London Company, which took possession of Sir Walter Raleigh's new world lands in 1606. He helped Sir Thomas Smythe reform the company in 1609 and took over for Smythe as Treasurer (chief executive officer of the company) in 1619. He promoted the policy of "headrights," which granted fifty acres to individuals who settled in the company's new world dominion and the establishment of a general assembly to improve administration of the colony. The colony's eventual success is widely attributed to Sandys' innovative measures.

Introduction

———•—•———

For there are no Examples so frequent in History, both Sacred and Prophane, as those of Men withdrawing themselves, and their Obedience, from the Jurisdiction they were born under, and the Family or Community they were bred up in, and setting up new Governments in other places; from whence sprang all that number of petty Common-wealths in the beginning of Ages, and which always multiplied, as long as there was room enough, till the stronger, more fortunate swallowed the weaker; and those great ones again breaking to pieces, dissolved into lesser Dominions.

—John Locke, Paragraph 115, *The Second Treatise of Government*

———•—•———

T HE BIRTH OF VIRGINIA'S ARISTOCRACY explains how the first civil society formed in Virginia, what purposes it served, who its members were, and what happened to it as it aged.

The self-transformation of its leading families into an "aristocracy" was the final stage in the development of Virginia's first civil society. There was more to their transformation than their ongoing acquisition of wealth and political power. Virginia's aristocracy formed after—and because of—the seldom-mentioned transfer of allegiance by Colonel Richard Lee II from his squabbling, fragmented community to a distant English Lord. After eighty years of growth and division, the descendents of the men who formed and filled Virginia's first civil society decided more or less en masse to surrender their natural sovereignty and to become part of a hereditary social system. Why would they do this? Some may have done so because they were vain. Others may simply have followed their neighbors. Whatever the particulars, a suitable general answer lies in the end result, which was a mechanism that preserved and perpetuated the community at large while benefiting the heirs of Virginia's patriarchs.

The body of the text is a narrative that sets the stage for Lee to make his puzzling submission. It remembers the efforts that were expended to establish a colony in the Virginia wilderness. It recounts the enlightened moments when the Virginia Company's frustrated leaders endorsed the concept of private property and authorized the creation of America's first legislature. It highlights the forty years needed by Virginia's emerging gentry to gain control of the colonial government and the power to sell their tobacco to a world market. It explains the change that occurred when Charles II gained the English throne in 1660—how his advisors under the direction of his calculating brother implemented policies to channel the wealth of the colony into their impoverished king's pocket and how this conflicted with Virginia's autocratic governor who was doing the same thing for *himself*. It introduces Thomas, 2nd Lord Culpeper and examines his motives and methods in gaining a share of Virginia's wealth. And it shows how Culpeper's death opened the way for his son-in-law, the debt-ridden 5th Lord Fairfax, to take possession of Culpeper's Virginia properties. Fairfax's frustrating efforts to collect rents on his Northern Neck Proprietary bring the reader at last to Colonel Lee.

Society's formation in Virginia takes on new significance when one recognizes that the process as it unfolded in this new world setting bore no clear resemblance to the process theorized by the political "scientists" who were writing on the subject at that time in England.

Thomas Hobbes published *Leviathan* (1651) shortly after the final royalist defeat in the English civil war. He acclaimed his analysis of man in society as the beginning of modern Politics Science, a discipline that Aristotle had invented two thousand years before. John Locke incorporated many of Hobbes' misconceptions about the process in which civil society forms into two treatises on government. The first of these contained his refutation of Sir Robert Filmer's *patriarchalism*. His 2nd *Treatise of Government* rationalized his claim that the authority of the state derives from the sovereignty of the people and that it is their right to define their common good and make law to accomplish it by the will of their *majority*. Locke published his *Two Treatises* on the eve of the Glorious Revolution (1689). In doing so he provided the theoretical foundation for the constitutional monarchy that Parliament established after the abdication of James II and for the political revolution that produced the United States of America.

The fragmented social construct that developed in Virginia was one of many unintended by-products of the Virginia Company's ongoing effort to create a profit-generating business. While the birth of Virginia's aristocracy is little more than a footnote in this perennial enterprise, it is interesting because of the seemingly inexplicable act of Colonel Lee.

Lee's acknowledgment of the Fairfax line as his liege lords was an expression of a new frame of mind. With this seemingly unnecessary act of self-submission, Lee transferred his allegiance from the squabbling amalgam that surrounded him in Virginia to a hereditary hierarchy that ascended ultimately to the King of England. In short order, Lee's social peers followed him with their own transfers of allegiance. These voluntary avowals changed the way Virginia's leading men and their families saw themselves. Where they had been members of the most privileged class of *colonials*, after their submission to the Lords Fairfax they were members of Mother England's most exclusive socio-political network. They conducted themselves in this proud estate—and sustained the rule of the English Monarch—until their impertinent kinsman declared American independence seventy-six years later.

Money is arguably the most important character in this story. It tracks through all six phases of the colony's development:

1. **Colonization (1587–1618):** during which time those who held the charters to the lands in Virginia undertook to find wealth in their new world wilderness.
2. **Sandys' Commonwealth (1619–1624):** during which time the London Council of the Virginia Company enacted Edwin Sandys' plan to create wealth by encouraging industrious settlers to pursue their own profit-generating business interests.
3. **First Royal Commonwealth (1625–1652):** during which time the King of England authorized his agents to appoint leading colonials to prestigious posts and to help them build wealth in exchange for their cooperation.
4. **Virginia Commonwealth (1653–1660):** during which time the "Tuckahoes" of Virginia's Tidewater organized the colony's government on the lines of Parliament's new republican system—in which the legislative branch of the government dominated its executive.
5. **Second Royal Commonwealth (1661–1700):** during which time a conflict developed between the governor of Virginia and his lieutenants and the Kings of England and their ministers, all of whom sought to manipulate the instruments of the colony's government to enrich themselves.
6. **The Old Dominion (1701–1776):** during which time members of Virginia's "aristocracy" counseled the King on matters of state, but ruled in their own counties.

If there is a hero in this story it is Sir Edwin Sandys (pronounced *sands*). Sandys' great accomplishment tends to be overshadowed by the corruption that proliferated during his administration and caused the Virginia Company to fail shortly after he completed his term as its Treasurer. Although he failed as an administrator, this failure does not diminish his standing as a political philosopher and social visionary.

Under Sandys' leadership, the Virginia Company's Jamestown colony transformed from a floundering *commune* into a thriving marketplace. Sandys orchestrated this transformation by harnessing the industry of individuals in pursuit of private profit. That is, he promoted the common good by giving individuals means to pursue their own interests. He did this by providing settlers who paid their own way to his company's new world colony fifty acres of land and the right to participate in a general assembly where they could make the laws of their community. Civil society in Virginia grew on these foundations.

Sandys was right in his belief that commonwealth is a necessary condition for prosperity—and hence for civil society. He was wrong to think that the common good it would promote would benefit every member of the community. The story told in the following pages confirms that the Jamestown colony began with a stratified social system and that it continued that way throughout its lifespan. The *body politic* that constituted Virginia's civil society never included the community's tenants, servants, or itinerants. As the colony grew, the benefits of its government, the authority of its administration and the prosperity that accompanied private industry all accrued to the individuals who controlled its land and thus its wealth. After fourscore years, the primary beneficiaries of this prosperity ennobled themselves as a class by forming a hereditary system. In doing this, the people at the top of Virginia's societal pyramid conferred upon themselves the consummate social benefit—perpetual supremacy.

Thomas Jefferson believed that this hierarchical system would eventually undermine the *republican* government of his newly independent state. To prevent this, he devised a plan to move control of the colony from it colonial oligarchy to a class of yeoman farmers that was forming in the state's western lands. Jefferson failed in his effort, but his objective was accomplished in stages after the American Revolution. The final chapter of the book reconstructs Jefferson's subtle plan.

ONE

Colonization

———•••———

Establishing a self-supporting colony in the wilderness of Virginia proved to be costly both in terms of treasure and human life. The early failures of the enterprise are often attributed to the characteristics of the "adventurers" who carried the project forward. The people, however, were only part of the problem. Colonizing Virginia was a business venture organized and superintended by men who were risking their wealth—and in some instances their lives—in an effort to gain what they hoped would be substantial *profits*. Unfortunately, they had no sure idea how to do this. Some expected to duplicate the success of Spain, which became rich by plundering an American civilization to the south. These hopes were dashed when neither gold nor other precious commodities were found in Virginia. Stagnation and hardship defined the venture until John Rolfe discovered a product that could be produced profitably in the Virginia Company's new world dominion. Profits generated by the production of tobacco secured the fate of the colony, not because they enriched its investors, but rather because they stimulated the formation of a marketplace. The colony acquired the wherewithal to succeed in 1616 when it was reorganized in a way that facilitated the growth of this marketplace.

———•••———

ENGLAND'S COLONIAL INTERESTS developed apace with the power of her navy. By the time her intrepid seamen vanquished Spain's first invading armada, Sir Walter Raleigh had already made three attempts to seed a colony in the vast territory defined in his royal grant. Sir Walter's inspiration to colonize the New World no doubt came from his half-brother, Sir Humphrey Gilbert, who in 1578 obtained a patent from Queen Elizabeth authorizing him to take possession of "any remote barbarous and heathen lands not possessed by any Christian prince or people." Sir Humphrey drowned in 1583 while exploring Newfoundland. Sir Walter renewed his half-brother's patent the following year. In his *Notes on Virginia*, in answer to Query XIII, Thomas Jefferson reported that Queen Elizabeth licensed Sir Walter, in her letter-patent dated 25 March 1584, "to search for remote heathen lands, not inhabited by Christian people" and granted him "all soil within 200 leagues of the places where his people should, within six years, make their dwellings or abidings."

Sir Walter wisely promoted his colonial venture as part of England's national interest, which focused increasingly on countering Spain's imperial expansion. He seasoned his promotion with talk of spreading God's word among the heathens. These advertisements notwithstanding, Sir Walter's primary concern was to find *treasure*. The colonization of America was at bottom a profit-seeking business enterprise. Sir Walter began his chapter of this perennial enterprise within a month of receiving his patent.

Early in April 1584, he ordered two ships to cross the Atlantic. When they reached Florida, they were to turn north and follow the coastline until they reached what is today the Outer Banks of North Carolina. There the ships' captains were instructed to find a site suitable to establish a colony. Sir Walter, having been knighted by Elizabeth I early in 1585, named this new land "Virginia" in honor of his queen. In April 1585, he sent out the first company of English settlers under the command of his cousin, Sir Richard Grenville. As Raleigh's men variously tried to displace, convert, and eradicate the

Sir Walter Raleigh (1552–1618)

Indians who inhabited the area, hostilities broke out between the intruders and the Indians, and this settlement failed. Sir Francis Drake rescued the survivors of the doomed settlement on his visit in 1586. Subsequent efforts to revive the colony were unsuccessful.

The cost of colonizing his wilderness province proved more than Sir Walter could bear alone. "He therefore," said Jefferson, "by deed bearing the date 7 March 1589, by the name of Sir Walter Raleigh, Chief of Assancomac (probably Accomac), alias Windacoia, alias Virginia, granted to Thomas Smith and others, in consideration of their adventuring certain sums of money, liberty to trade with His new country free from all customs and taxes for seven years."[1] Sir Walter thus generated what may have been the only revenue he derived from his adventure in Virginia. Since the province had no colonies with which to trade, his business partners did not achieve even this dubious level of success.

Raleigh was sent to the Tower of London in 1603 for being a conspirator in what is known today as the "Main Plot." The purported objective of this conspiracy was to replace England's newly crowned king, James Stuart of Scotland, with his cousin Arabella. The plot's leader, Lord Cobham, was reported to be negotiating with the Spanish court for a large sum of money that he and Raleigh planned to use to fund the rebellion. Raleigh was found guilty of the charges despite seemingly weak evidence. This may explain why James spared his life. He was confined to the Tower, however, for the next thirteen years.

One Grant for Two Colonies

With Raleigh out of the picture, others sought grants to develop colonies. "Some gentlemen and merchants," Jefferson stated, "supposing that by the attainder of Sir Walter Raleigh the grant to him was forfeited, petitioned King James for a new grant of Virginia to them."[2] James responded in 1606. His letter-patent of 10 April grants eight patentees and others who were unnamed the right to establish two colonies in Virginia.[3] The first colony was under the authority of a syndicate of London merchants and gentlemen. The second was under the authority of a syndicate of Plymouth-area merchants and gentlemen. Both of these enterprises were to be overseen by a thirteen-member council appointed by the king. This governing body, known as the Council of Virginia, formed the core of the Virginia Company. As a royal charter, the expenses associated with launching the venture were to be borne by the Crown.

Five days before Christmas 1606, the council dispatched a fleet of three ships with 120 "adventurers" under the command of Christopher Newport. Newport sailed with sealed instructions not to be opened until he reached his destination.

Newport entered the Chesapeake Bay and reached the mouth of a great tributary, which he christened the James River in honor of his king. About this time he opened the council's instructions, which described the form of the colony's government. It was to consist of a panel of thirteen men whose names appeared in the document. Among these were George Kendall, who would be executed for sowing discord in the colony; Richard Hunt, a clergyman who is thought to have carried the typhoid fever that decimated the company's first settlement; and John Smith, whose inspired leadership would carry the colony through its second winter. Edward-Maria Wingfield, a large investor and core member of the Virginia Company, was elected the council's president. It was Wingfield in his capacity as president of the colonial council who selected the site where the colony was planted. He chose an isthmus with a deep water anchorage sixty miles upstream from the bay.

Wingfield was a decorated veteran, having campaigned against the Spanish in the Low Countries in the late 1580s. During his military service he developed a reputation as a strong leader. Being a forceful leader was not enough, however, to overcome the hostile conditions he encountered in Virginia. First among them was a drought, recently characterized by historians as the worst in 800 years. As crops withered and fresh water grew scarce, disease and starvation set in. Attacks by the Indians who lived in the area posed another life-threatening problem. Wingfield's attempt to overcome these problems with hard work and increased vigilance sapped the waning strength of his command and further undermined its morale. Five months after landing, Wingfield was arrested and removed from his post.

The Failure of Communalism

The rapid deterioration in the condition of the colony suggests that another detrimental factor was also at work. Noted historian Virginius Dabney framed the issue in these words: "[T]he early enthusiasm soon wore off, with the result that many began shirking. One of the best reasons was that a *communal plan*, based on principles similar to today's communism, had been prescribed for the settlers before they left England. Under it, property and produce were owned jointly. The results were devastating."[4] (emphasis added)

"Our men were destroyed with cruel diseases as Swellings, Fluxes, Burning Fevers, and by wars," acting governor George Percy reported in 1610, "and some departed suddenly, but for the most part, they died of mere famine. There were never Englishmen left in a foreign country in such misery as we were in this new discovered Virginia."[5] John Smith was elected president of the council in September 1608. During his twelve-month tenure, he managed to ameliorate this problem by making food-gathering a priority. Unfortunately for the colonists, Smith was forced to surrender his post and return to England in October 1609 after being severely injured in an accidental discharge of powder while returning to Jamestown from an expedition upriver.

In the meantime the king, vexed by the staggering cost of the venture, rechartered his royal company and transferred control of the colony—and liability for funding it—from the Crown to private

Sir George Somers' Third Supply Fleet sailing for Jamestown, 1609

investors who would now have to risk their own capital in pursuit of New World profit. This new joint-stock company exercised its authority by appointing Sir Thomas Gates to serve as governor.

Gates set off for Virginia in June 1609 in a fleet of nine ships under the command of Sir George Somers, admiral and one of the Virginia Company's principal investors. Besides badly need supplies, the fleet carried 500 new colonists. As it turned west from the Azores, it encountered a fierce storm, which continued to blow for three days. During the gale, the fleet divided and the two pinnaces crossing in tow were lost.

The flagship of the fleet, which carried Gates and Somers, was the *Sea Venture*. The *Sea Venture* had been in the water only a short time before the voyage. Sir George Somers had ordered and paid the 1,500 pounds it cost to construct and had superintended its design. It had been built specifically to ferry men and supplies from England to the Virginia Company's New World colony. Because it was new, however, its caulk had not yet cured. The three-day storm therefore washed out its caulk and opened its seams to a torrent of

Sir George Somers Discovering Bermuda the Hard Way, 1609

leaks. In danger of foundering, Admiral Somers managed to steer the stricken vessel onto a reef in what is now St. George's Bay on the northeastern coast of Bermuda. All aboard survived the storm.

Stranded on the uninhabited island, Gates and Somers fell into

Sir Thomas Gates, Governor of Virginia, 1610

dispute over who should command. Gates claimed he had come into his authority as governor of the colony. Somers claimed he retained authority as admiral of the fleet. Unable to resolve the matter, they split into two camps and proceeded to build two ships. Somers' camp built a thirty-ton pinnace called *Patience*. Gates' supervised construction of an eighty-ton barque, which he christened *Deliverance*. Ten months later, Somers commanded the successful passage of the two ships to Virginia. They reached the colony on 24 May 1610.

"What a miserable condition we found the Colony at our arrival there from the Bermudas," Gates' secretary Ralphe Hamor reported, "not living above threescore persons therein, and those scarce able to go alone." In ten months nearly 500 colonists had perished. Why? "The reason hereof is at hand," Hamor explained, "for formerly, when our people were fed out of the common store and labored jointly in the manuring of the ground, and planting corn, glad was that man who could slip from his labor. Nay the most honest of them…would not take so much faithful and true pains in a week, as now he will do in a day. Neither cared they for the increase, presuming that howsoever their harvest prospered, the general store must maintain them."[6] Since they had not sown, they could not reap.

Gates and Martial Law

Now in command, Gates set about making straight what he found crooked. His plan for doing this was to implement the new system of government that the London Council had authorized prior to his departure the previous year. In its *Laws Divine, Moral and Martial*, the council instructed Gates "to proceed by Martial Law according to your commission as of most dispatch and terror and fittest for this government.…In all matters of Civil Justice," it continued, "you shall find it [most] proper and useful for your government to proceed rather as a Chancellor than as a Judge, rather upon natural right and equity than upon the niceness and letter of the law."[7] Following these instructions, Gates instituted what was to be eight years of martial law under which severe, sometimes-lethal punishments were exacted for "shirking," "irreligion," and behavior deemed disruptive to the good order and morale of the company.

Gates governed the colony from May 1610 until his immediate superior, Thomas West, 3rd Lord De La Warr, relieved him in June of that year. West sent Gates back to England shortly after his arrival to collect supplies and recruit new adventurers for the colony. West's health began to deteriorate shortly after he reached the colony, and he was forced to return to England in March 1611. West left Sir George Percy, an investor named in the Virginia Company's 1609 charter, to oversee the colony until Gates returned. Gates completed his mission and resumed his post in September 1611. In addition to badly needed supplies, he brought from England 300 new colonists. Gates governed until he left the colony for good in March 1614.

Gates' strict regimen enabled the tottering colony to survive, but it stifled development of private initiative. Sir Thomas Dale, who succeeded Gates, alluded to this problem in his letter to an unknown member of the London Council dated 10 June 1613. "Now consider this people," he wrote, "and give your judgment what should be become of them did I not compel them to work. Oh sir my heart bleeds when I think what men we have here; did I not carry a severe hand over them they would starve one another by breaking open houses and chests to steal a pottle of corn from their poor brother, and when they have stolen that, the poor man must starve."[8]

Captain John Smith shared Dale's views that the colonists' ethics and the lack of private economic incentives were the problem. In her introduction to part 5 of *Captain John Smith*, Karen Ordahl Kupperman observed: "Jamestown... was a money-making venture though with royal support, and in the early years everyone in the colony worked for the company. Captain Smith saw the flaw in such a plan earlier than most."[9] She added in a footnote comment that Smith's "argument is that you cannot build a new society with nothing but the refuse of England."[10]

Dale made his complaint in response to criticism he had received from the London Council about the underperformance of the colony as a business venture. Dale pointedly redirected blame for this back to the council itself. At the same time, however, he took steps to ameliorate the problem. According to Hamor, Dale "has taken a new course, throughout the whole Colony, by which means, the general store (apparel only excepted) shall not be charged with anything; and... he has allotted to every man in the Colony, three English Acres of clear Corn ground, which every man is to mature and tend, being in the nature of Farmers... and they are not [to be] called unto any service or labor belonging to the Colony, more than one month in the year, which shall neither be in seed time."[11] Colonists were also required to contribute two barrels of corn each year to maintain a reserve to feed new settlers until they could harvest their own first crop.

In this way, Dale made the first connection between the colony's chronic food shortages and the mode in which its lands were held. Forests had to be cleared, and cleared land had to be planted. Planted fields had to be tended. To get settlers to perform this back-breaking work, Sir Thomas proposed that all settlers, whatever their rank, grow their own food on *their own land*. The London Council advanced on this line in 1616 when it issued the Virginia Company's first dividends to its investors. Lacking funds for cash disbursements, the council authorized distributions of land in *hundreds*—enough land to support 100 households—to certain of the company's principal investors.[12] These disbursements created the first *private* property in Virginia.

These events reveal that awareness was developing among the leaders of the enterprise that for the colony to accomplish the Virginia Company's objectives, it needed a more dynamic system. Modern historian and essayist Louis Rubin added that the Virginia Company needed to attract "a generally better sort of colonist—men and women of industry and responsibility."[13] The company soon undertook to do this by offering prospective settlers a better *economic* opportunity. This change in approach provided a fitting introduction for John Rolfe.

John Rolfe's Vital Discovery

During John Rolfe's eleven-year residence in Virginia he demonstrated skills as a farmer and a merchant, both of which contributed to his accumulation of wealth and fame. His contribution to the success of the colony as a business venture was on a par with that of Sir Edwin Sandys. Rolfe made his place by cultivating the first crop of commercially viable tobacco. He grew this crop from seeds he had with him from Plymouth, England, when he boarded the *Sea*

The Baptism of Pocahontas at Jamestown, Virginia, 1614

Venture in early June 1609. His daughter was born on the island of Bermuda after Somers grounded the ship there in mid-June 1609. She, whom he named Bermuda, died there while the island-built transports were being constructed. In early May 1610, Rolfe sailed on to Jamestown with his wife, who died a short time after their arrival. Two years after her death, Rolfe provided the missing piece of colonial Virginia's economic puzzle: After harvesting Virginia's first crop of Orinoco tobacco, he married Pocahontas. Their marriage was followed by three years of peace between Virginia's colonials and the Powhatan Indians.

Tobacco was indigenous to Virginia, but the species that grew there had small leaves and a bitter taste that made it unpalatable to Europeans. Rolfe's seeds were of the *Nicotiana tabacum* species, which was a large-leafed, sweet-tasting tobacco cultivated by the Spanish in the West Indies. It proved to be popular enough among the colonists that several of the colony's farmers began to cultivate it. Edmund Morgan reported that the colony shipped its first

Pocahontas at the Court of King James I, 1617

cargo of tobacco to England in 1617.[14] John Smith claimed that it sold at three shillings per pound, which was well below the rate commanded for the Spanish-grown variety. The planting of tobacco spread rapidly after that with "the weed" being sown at one point even in the streets of Jamestown.

By 1616, the company had established four settlements and had begun to build a network of communities called "plantations" on land granted to the company's shareholders and agents. Land ownership and community creation policies allowed the company to attract a different kind of adventurer. These were men, some with families, who came to Virginia to grow tobacco and to profit from selling it. When enough of these enterprising men and women established themselves, the colony began to transform itself from a paramilitary outpost that operated under martial law into a *commonwealth* governed by its inhabitants. In this way, the introduction of private land ownership marked the beginning of an important new phase in the colony's development.

TWO

The Commonwealth Period

———•—•———

Sir Thomas Dale pointed the Virginia Company's London Council in the right direction by noting the connection between the quantity of food the colony produced and the mode in which its lands were held. The London Council took a significant first step forward when it granted private ownership of land to certain of its most important investors. Under the leadership of Sir Edwin Sandys, the company made private land ownership a general policy in 1618 when it instituted a "headrights" system, which provided fifty acres of land to every individual who paid his own way to the colony and resided there three years. The opportunity to earn profits planting tobacco and selling it to the company's "magazine" attracted entrepreneurial emigrants. Sandys promoted the success of their private businesses by creating a *general assembly* in which they could define their common good and make laws to improve their marketplace. Joining together to do this, the headmen of the colony's earliest "plantations" formed its first *civil society*.

———•—•———

T HE COMMONWEALTH that formed in Virginia allowed individuals to pursue their private interests as members of a community. Unlike the commonwealths theorized later by Thomas Hobbes and John Locke, the one that formed in Virginia depended on a symbiotic relationship in which the well-being of the community rested on the success its members achieved in their *private* endeavors. Their success depended, in turn, on the ability of the community to provide a marketplace where they could buy and sell goods, procure needed services, and fulfill their needs as social creatures. Virginia's planters shared a *common communal interest* in the sense that they recognized the need for products they could sell at a profit and a market where they could be sold. They promoted their common good by striving to provide these essential components for their economic success. They promoted social harmony by adhering to *common ways*. By doing these things, a group of individuals struggling to survive in a wilderness beyond the civilized world formed what qualifies here as a *civil society*.

Both Hobbes and Locke would later argue that civil society forms when individuals purposefully bind themselves one with another into a single encompassing *body politic*. Locke argued that it was the right of this political body to define the common good and make the law to accomplish it by the will of its majority. In the real world of Virginia, however, civil society *emerged* as members of the community pursued their private business interests. Both Hobbes and Locke were wrong on another important point. In Virginia, membership in the body politic was open only to those who, by paying an entry fee, acquired the opportunity to earn business profits. That is, civil society in Virginia was a by-product of the effort to build the marketplace needed to sustain the commonwealth.

The directors of the Virginia Company had the objective of creating a profit-generating business. In 1606 they had no inkling that they might also create a civil society, that a thriving marketplace was needed to sustain it, or that it would grow out of private enterprise. In the absence of this knowledge, it was impossible for them to formulate the concept of *commonwealth*. They settled instead for a Lockean oath that bound the members of their settlement to be true and faithful servants to His Majesty and to his majesty's Council of Virginia. Under the circumstances, it is not surprising that this community remained an amalgam of disjointed, sometimes openly hostile, segments.

The directors of the enterprise seem to have approached their work with good intentions. But they did not know how to generate profits. Nor did they know how to configure their colony so the people they sent to do this could survive. They squandered thousands of lives in the process of learning these things.

Corporate Profits
and the Common Good

The company's investors had been led to expect rapid returns on their investments. By 1618 they were becoming impatient. In increasing numbers, they refused to fulfill their financial subscriptions. And they hastened the company's demise by embroiling it in lawsuits charging fraud and mismanagement. James I was another looming adversary. While the documents his ministers prepared suggest that he was concerned with the well-being of his subjects, he did little to protect them or to improve their lot before (or after) revoking the company's charter in 1624.

The soldiers who accompanied the colonists were company employees and under orders to explore its new dominion and to establish commercial relations with the "naturals." They were not there, in other words, to feed the colony. The company's paying customers, identified in its records as "private people," had purchased the right to hunt for Virginia's treasures. They had no formal obligation—and no inclination—to spend their time building the company's settlement or growing its food. The men whose passage the company paid owed a service to the company, but few of these men had useful skills. The few artisans the company did recruit to build its settlements probably found the social barriers that separated them from their traveling companions stifling. Lack of *esprit de corps* would have aggravated morale problems spawned by the dismal prospect these workingmen faced in their new uncivilized world.

As originally framed, the enterprise was deficient according to the interests of each of these parties. Not only did it fail to return a profit to the corporation and its investors, it also did not exist in a way that allowed individual adventurers to prosper. Under the royal charter it received in 1606, the company received a monopoly on the colony's trade.[15] It was to pay the Crown a duty of 2.5 percent on each of its commercial transactions. For transactions involving individuals who were not English subjects, the company was to pay the Crown a 5 percent commission. The problem with this plan was that the cost of establishing trading centers was greater than the revenue they generated. The king made up the difference for three years, and then changed the company's charter.

The directors of the rechartered company addressed the problem themselves in 1618 after an audit revealed that it had lost almost all of its 75,000 pounds of working capital. Responding to this shocking news, the council endorsed a new business plan framed by Sir Edwin Sandys.

Sandys had confirmed his progressive sentiments in the final years of Elizabeth's reign by writing a tract in which he espoused religious tolerance. In a display of political shrewdness, he supported James VI's accession to the English throne following the death of Elizabeth. James rewarded his support by knighting him in 1603. Sitting in the new king's first parliament, Sandys established himself as a political progressive by advocating the right of prisoners to counsel and by opposing commercial monopolies, which were then proliferating in England.

Sandys' Idea of Commonwealth

The Virginia Company's colonial venture provided a fitting outlet for Sandys' enlightened sentiments and progressive energies. He applied them as an investor and a member of the company's governing council by leading an effort to hold ballot votes on policy decisions made by the council.

Sandys' objective for the company was, in effect, to complete the transformation of its colony into a commonwealth. Following his lead, the council drafted a new set of instructions for Governor-elect George Yeardley. These instructions, dated 18 November 1618, opened with this hope-filled introduction: "Our former cares and Endeavors have been chiefly bent to the procuring and sending people to plant in Virginia so *to prepare a way and to lay a foundation whereon A flourishing State might in process of time by the blessing of Almighty God be raised*...because our intent is to Ease all the Inhabitants of Virginia forever of all taxes and public burdens as much as may be and to take away all occasion of oppression and corruption we have thought fit to begin (according to the laudable Example of the most famous Common Wealths both past and present) to allot and lay out a Convenient portion of public lands for the maintenance and support as well of Magistracy and officers as of other public charges both here and there from time to time arising."[16](emphasis added)

The council instructed Governor-elect Yeardley to lay out one 3,000-acre parcel to be called the "Governor's Land" and a like amount to be called the "Companies Land." Yeardley was directed to set fifty persons whose passage to Virginia the company paid *prior* to Sir Thomas Dale's departure (in 1616) to tend the "Governor's Land." Persons whose passage the company had paid *after* Dale's departure were to tend the "Companies Land." Profits earned on produce from the Governor's Land were to be equally divided between the tenants and the Governor. Profits earned on produce from the Companies Land were to be equally divided between the tenants and the Company.

The council went on to implement Thomas Dale's earlier recommendation by instructing Yeardley to grant 100 acres to every colonist who both paid his own passage to Virginia prior to the departure of Thomas Dale and remained in Virginia at least three years—or died in the interim. Those who came to Virginia at the company's expense prior to Dale's departure and who had remained three years in the company's service were also to receive 100 acres. The council then implemented the first of Sandys' two great policy innovations: private property. "We do hereby ordain that all such persons as since Sir Thomas Dale have at their own charges been transported thither to inhabit and so continued as aforesaid there be allotted and set out upon a first division fifty acres of land to them and their heirs forever for their personal Adventure paying a free rent of one Shilling yearly in manner aforesaid...."[17]

This land grant was to become known as a "headright." Sandys was right to promote it. During its eighty-five-year life span, it produced a steady influx of the prosperous, industrious people needed to sustain Virginia's development as a commonwealth. Sandys reached out to enterprising people who were less prosperous with a different policy: "[A]ll persons which since the going away of the said Sir Thomas Dale have been transported thither at the Companies charges or which hereafter shall be so transported be placed as *tenants on the Companies lands for term of seven years....* We do therefore hereby ordain that all such persons as of their own Voluntary Will and authority shall remove into Virginia without any Grant from us in a great general and Quartering Court in writing under our seal shall be deemed (as they are) to be occupiers of our Land that is to say of the Common Lands of us the said Treasurer and Company and shall pay unto us for the said occupying of our Land one full fourth part of the profits thereof until *such time as the same shall be granted unto them by us in manner aforesaid.*"[18] (emphasis added.)

This provision for tenants and rent formed the basis for the indentured servitude through which most of Virginia's early settlers passed on their way to becoming citizens in Sandys' commonwealth. The council's 18 November missive concluded with instructions to promote industry other than "husbandry or other rural business" by providing artisans who might start such businesses a house and four acres of land in any of the colony's settlements and to do a survey of these areas so its land grants could be properly established and maintained.

THREE

Civil Society in Virginia

The concept of *commonwealth* did not originate with Sir Edwin
Sandys, but Sandys deserves the lion's share of the credit for the
transformation of the colony of Virginia into one. Sandys would
qualify today as a "progressive" for using the power of his position as
a member of the Virginia Company's London Council and then as
the company's Treasurer [Chief Operating Officer] to create a better
functioning social organism. Sandys had what boiled down to a two-
part plan: 1) attract more industrious people to the colony, and 2)
help them succeed in their private business enterprises. The first civil
society to form in Virginia did so on Sandys' two basic principles.
These *economic* components distinguished Sandys' social philosophy
from those of his renowned successors, Thomas Hobbes and John
Locke. Sandys' theory proved unlike theirs in other fundamental
respects. Membership in his society did not open, for example, to
every colonist. Nor did the good it sought uniformly benefit its
inhabitants. Sandys' system did however promote the most basic and
essential interest of everyone in the Virginia Company's tottering
settlement. That is, by promoting the business interests of its leading
men, Sandys' system helped to generate the profits that the colonial
organism—and hence its individual cells—needed to survive. Thanks
to Sandys' landownership policy and his participatory system of
government, by 1622 the colony was feeding itself and exporting
thousands of tons of tobacco to mother England.

"A COMMON-WEALTH," in the words of Thomas Hobbes, "is said to be instituted, when a multitude of men do agree, and covenant, everyone, with everyone, that to whatsoever man, or assembly of men, shall be given by the major part, the right to present the person of them all, (that is to say, to be their representative;) everyone, as well he that voted for it, as that voted against it, shall authorize all the actions and judgments, of that man, or assembly of men, in the same manner, as if they were his own, to the end, to live peaceably amongst themselves, and be protected against other men."[19] Hobbes proceeded in *Leviathan* to define the body of men who join together in this covenant as a *body politic*.[20]

"It is not every compact," Locke added, "that puts an end to the State of Nature between men, but only this one of agreeing together mutually to enter into one community, and make one body politic."[21] "And it is not without reason," he continued, "that he seeks out, and is willing to join in society with others who are already united, or have a mind to unite for the mutual preservation of their lives, liberties, and estates, which I call by the general name, *Property*.... The great and chief end therefore, of men uniting into Commonwealths, and putting themselves under government, is the preservation of their Property. To which in the State of Nature there are many things wanting."[22] (emphasis added)

Self-Government

Sandys, who formed his ideas long before either Hobbes or Locke published their discussions on society, did not have the benefit of their pre-enlightened meditations. Still, his system, driven as it was by necessity, had a *body politic*. It formed when Governor-elect George Yeardley[23] implemented Sandys' other great innovation: self-government. In its 18 November instructions, the council declared that the colony's government was to "benefit the people and strengthen the colony." Good government was, in other words, an essential part of Sandys' plan to build Virginia into a "flourishing state." It was to be "a laudable form of government by majestracy" with "just laws for the happy guiding and governing of the people there inhabiting like as we have already done for the well ordering of our Courts here...."[24] That is, Sandys wanted the colony's inhabitants to participate in making its laws as the members of the council did when making company policy.

Before Yeardley departed to take his post, the council therefore authorized him to establish a *General Assembly*. The document containing these instructions has been lost, but John Pory, Speaker of the first assembly, described it in his report on the proceedings of that august body: "[H]aving thus prepared them he [the Speaker of the General Assembly] read unto them [the burgesses] the *great Charter*, or commission of privileges, orders and laws, sent by Sir George Yeardley out of England. Here begin the laws drawn out of the instructions given by his Majesty's Counsel of Virginia in England to my lord La Warr, Captain Argall and Sir George Yeardley, knight."[25]

The "great Charter" outlined a government similar to the one defined two years later in the "Ordinances and Constitution of the Treasurer," which the council enacted on 24 July 1621. As stated in its preamble, the purpose of this constitution was "to settle such a form of government there, as may be the greatest benefit and comfort of the people" and "as also advancing of increase, strength, stability, and prosperity of the said colony." It declared that there were to be "two supreme councils in Virginia." The first, called the "Council of State," was to be "placed and displaced, from time to time, by us, the said Treasurer, Council, and Company, and our successors." The other, the "General Assembly," was to be like the Council of State and the company's London-based Council of Virginia in that "all matters shall be decided, determined, and ordered, by the greater part of the voices then present, reserving to the Governor always a negative voice." The assembly, which the

31

governor was to call once a year, was to consist of the governor and his five-man council and "two Burgesses out of every town, hundred, or other plantation, to be respectively chosen by the inhabitants."[26] It was to have "free power to treat, consult, and conclude, as well of all emergent occasions concerning the public weal of the colony and every part thereof, as also to make, ordain, and enact such general laws and orders, for the benefit of the said colony, and the good government thereof." The London Council went on to stipulate that both governing bodies imitate and follow England's form of government, including its laws, customs, and judicial system. In other words, England's common law, upon which rested the rights and liberties of Englishmen in Britain, was to apply across the pond.

The First General Assembly

Virginia's first General Assembly convened on 30 July 1619 and ended on 4 August. Pory confirmed to the company's directors that it acted "to preserve the peace and order" in their emerging commonwealth. The governor and his counselors, twenty-two delegates from eleven precincts, a Clerk and a Sargeant at Arms began with a prayer "that it would please God to guide and sanctify all our proceedings to his own glory and the good of this plantation." Having invoked the blessings of the Deity, each member of the assembly, "took the oath of Supremacy, and the entered the Assembly."

The proceedings stalled when Captain Warde rose to swear his oath. It was Speaker Pory who objected that he had no right to participate in the meeting on the grounds that his plantation was part of Captain Martin's and that "he was but a limb or member of him." This controversy was resolved when Captain Warde agreed to "procure from the Treasurer, Council and Company in England a commission lawfully to plant himself and his Company as the chiefs of other plantations had done." Governor Yeardley then directed the

Scene VI: "The First General Assembly of Virginia" from The Jamestown Story, *as told in the Grace Street Windows of Miller and Rhoades, Richmond, Virginia, 1619*

assembly to determine whether Captain Martin should have a place in the assembly on the grounds that his patent exempted him "from that equality and uniformity of laws and orders which the great charter says are to extend over the whole Colony, but also from diverse such laws as we must be enforced to make in the General Assembly." Completing this examination, the assembly decided that Captain Martin and his company should be admitted only if he agreed to "submit himself to the form of government as all others did ... otherwise they were to be utterly excluded as being spies rather than loyal Burgesses, because they had offered themselves to be assistant at the making of laws which both themselves and those whom they represented might choose whether they would obey or not." The assembly then summoned "our loving friend, Captain

Martin, Esquire, Master of the Ordinance" to appear before it "to treat and confer with us about some matters of special importance which concerns both us and the whole Colony [and] yourself." This closed the matter pending Captain Martin's appearance.

The Speaker then read "the great Charter, or commission of privileges, orders and laws...which for the more ease of the committees, having [been] divided into four books, he read the former two the same forenoon for expeditions sake...and so they were referred to the perusal of two committees...." These two committees, each having eight members, then retired to complete their deliberations.

Pory summarized the assembly's business under four headings. The first, the examination of the great charter of orders, laws and privileges, was already in process. Remaining to be taken up were "the instructions given by the Counsel in England to my Lord La Warr, Captain Argall or Sir George Yeardley, [which] might conveniently be put on the habit of laws," enactment of "laws [that] might issue out of the private conceit of any of the Burgesses, or any other of the Colony," and drafting "petitions...fit to be sent home to England." The assembly's first session ended with its decision to honor Governor Yeardley's request to lead the remaining members of the assembly in dealing with the second of these four matters.

The second session began with a report from the committee, which had examined the so-called "first book" of the great charter. This led to the framing of its first set of petitions. The first pertained to the London Council's instructions to create the two 3,000 acre parcels to be called the "Governor's Land" and the "Company's Land." The assembly requested permission to do this in such a way as not to alter the patents of "ancient planters by former governors that had from the Company received commission so to do, might not now after so much labor and cost, and so many years of habitation be taken from them."

The assembly's second petition pertained to the findings of the committee that had examined the second book. In this petition, the assembly asked the company to "send men hither to occupy their lands belonging to the four incorporations, as well as for their own benefit and profit as for the maintenance of the Counsel of Estate, who are now to their extreme hindrance often drawn far from their private business...."

Petition for Equal Property Rights

The assembly then petitioned the council "that it be plainly expressed in the great commission (as indeed it is not)" that the ancient planters [meaning those who had paid their own passage to the colony prior to the departure of Thomas Dale] as well as those whose passage the company had paid, "may have their second, third and more divisions successively in as large and free manner as any other planters." That is, the assembly wanted the company to grant what amounted to the same *headrights* to settlers who arrived before 1616 as it now meant to give to newly arriving immigrants. The assembly wanted these grants made to all *male* children brought to the colony by its existing settlers and to *all children* born in Virginia. In a fourth petition, the assembly asked the London Council to establish a "Sub-Treasurer" who would reside in the colony and collect the company's rents and that the council "enjoin the said Sub-Treasurer not precisely according to the letter of the Charter to exact money of us (whereof we have none at all, as we have no mint), but the true value of the rent in commodity." In a fifth petition, the assembly asked the counsel to provide "workmen of all sorts" to build a "University and College." The final petition was a request to change the "savage name of Kiccowtan, and to give that incorporation as new name."

Having thus dealt with the issues that had arisen out of the examination of the first two books of the great charter, the assembly received the committees' reports on the charter's third and fourth books. In the opinions of the committees, these books were "perfect."

Governor Yeardley, however, thought it unwise, given the uncertain relations between the colonials and the naturals, to establish new plantations ten miles apart as the London Council had instructed.

The assembly turned then to the instructions given by the Counsel in England to Lord La Warr, Captain Argall and Sir George Yeardley. In its first enactment, the assembly established the price of tobacco "at three shillings the best and second sort at 18*d* the pound." The assembly went on to institute what amounted to a common code of conduct. It was to be illegal to injure or oppress Indians "whereby the present peace might be disturbed and ancient quarrels might be revived." Colonists who engaged in "idleness, gaming and drunkenness" would be subject to fines and penalties. "Excess in apparel" was likewise forbidden. The assembly instructed the colonials in dealing with the natives that "it were fit a house were build for them to lodge in apart by themselves, and lone inhabitants by no means to entertain them."

To lay a "surer foundation" for the conversion of the Indians to Christian Religion, each settlement was to obtain "by just means a certain number of the natives' children to be educated by them in true religion and civil course of life." To strengthen the Christian religion of the colonists themselves, the assembly ordained that "all persons whatsoever upon the Sabbath day shall frequent divine service and sermons both forenoon and afternoon, and all such as bear arms shall bring their pieces swords, boulder and shot. And every one that transgresses this law shall forfeit three shillings a time to the use of the church, all lawful and necessary impediments excepted. But if a servant in this case shall willfully neglect his Master's command, he shall suffer bodily punishment."

The assembly attempted to preserve the well-being of the colony's inhabitants by ordering "all and every household and householders to have in store for every servant he or they shall keep, and also for his or their own persons, whether they have any servants or no, one spare barrel of corn, to be delivered out yearly, either upon sale or exchange and need shall require."

Several measures were enacted to broaden the colony's agricultural economy. "About the plantation of mulberry trees," Pory reported, "be it enacted that every man as he is seated upon his division, do for seven years together, every year plant and maintain in growth six mulberry trees at the least...." The planting of silk-flax was likewise recommended on the chance that it would be "found a commodity." The same for hemp, "both English and Indian," and for English flax and aniseeds. The assembly directed that "every householder do yearly plant and maintain ten vines until they have attained to the art and experience of dressing a vineyard either by their own industry or by the instruction of some vigneron."[27]

A Common Communal Interest

By obliging all colonists to be modest, civil, prudent, and enterprising, the assembly sought to cultivate the kind of individual who was needed for their enterprise to succeed. Enacting measures that did this did not cause it to become a commonwealth. This happened when the men who had the largest investments in the venture endorsed the idea. They did this by taking their seats in the new assembly and by enacting laws to improve conditions and prospects for themselves and their comrades. This was after a fashion a social contract. While it did not exist in a Lockean form, the commitment by Virginia's headmen to shoulder the burden of government confirmed a *common communal interest* and their willingness to pursue a common good. This moment can therefore be described as the beginning of *civil society* in Virginia.

Neither then, nor later, however, did it include the people who formed the great majority of the general population.

The General Assembly provided a forum in which the few who were members of the colony's body politic could define a good that was common to *themselves* and to devise ways to accomplish it. In 1619, the interests of Virginia's headmen were not so different from those of the men beneath them. They all aspired to prosper and they all needed to stay alive to do that. Generating business profits was necessary to sustain the commonwealth and, therefore, for the survival of *all* its adventurers. In this abstract way, promoting the interests of Virginia's small closed civil society of headmen benefited everyone who lived in the community. But since the tangible benefits accrued to the proprietors of the businesses that generated the profits, pursuing the common good widened the distance that separated the fledgling commonwealth's social classes.

FOUR

From Commonwealth
to Collapse

—————•••—————

As the colonial cell grew, it divided. These divisions, which occurred
on physical, social, and economic lines, magnified during each
succeeding phase of the colony's development. The power wielded
by its first citizens continued to increase even as its population
fragmented. Serving in its legislature, the colony's leading men
superintended its defense, kept its peace, administered its justice,
and created economic opportunities that tended to benefit themselves. *Corruption also proliferated as the colony grew.* It was practiced
by the colony's leading citizens, by its lesser citizens, and by the
Virginia Company's own agents. Its greatest victim was the Virginia
Company itself, which in the course of its first fifteen years lost all
of its capital. As its financial condition deteriorated, the company's
ability to support its new world business declined and its investors grew increasingly adversarial. The company was dealt a final
devastating blow on 22 March 1622 when the Powhatan Indians
launched a coordinated attack on its settlements. Within two yeas
of this disaster, the King of England revoked the Virginia Company's charter and placed its colony under royal authority.

—————•••—————

COMMONWEALTH IN VIRGINIA was, in a sense, a fortuitous accident that had time to occur because entrepreneurial men and women—the most important participants in the migration Edwin Sandys directed between 1618 and 1623—continued to dare their lives on the chance that they would prosper in the New World. The company appealed to these enterprising individuals by offering them private ownership of land and an opportunity to profit through its cultivation. It promoted its own interests—to build a marketplace that it would control—by creating a forum in which its residents could define their interests and enact laws conducive to their accomplishment. These then were the fruits of the founding process: *private property, individual liberty to pursue private profit*, and a *common communal interest* defined in the pronouncements of the representatives of the colony's business owners. Without these things, commonwealth could not have formed in Virginia. With them, civil society appeared and there was economic growth and periods of (uneven) prosperity.

Conflict and Rebellion

There was also factionalism, political conflict, and rebellion. Why? Because the growth that fueled the profit-generating business upon which Virginia's commonwealth and civil society depended also activated division in much the same way a cell divides to grow.

The business venture that supported the colonization of Virginia encompassed a diversity of interests. In this sense, the organism that became Virginia's commonwealth was never the single "person" that Hobbes and Locke postulated. Rather it spanned *three* distinct classes of citizens each with progressively fewer prerogatives and prospects.

Its *first* class contained those individuals who paid their own passage to the colony. A few of these individuals may have been tradesmen, but most entered directly into the business of clearing land and planting tobacco. Not only were they engaged in for-profit business, as "freeholders" (individuals who owned at least fifty acres of land) they were also eligible to serve on juries, to hold public office, and to vote in public elections. They were, in other words, full members in Virginia's new body politic. Since they were eligible to participate in the legislative process in which the common good was defined, they wielded the power to amend the system in ways that best suited their interests.

Those whose passage the company paid did not enjoy the same prerogatives. Members of this *second* class of emigrants worked as tenants on the company's land until they fulfilled their obligations as debtors to the company. During this period of service, which could last up to seven years, they shared the revenue they earned from the crops they raised on the company's land with their landlord. Virginius Dabney reports that they had the right to vote,[28] but since they were not freeholders, they could not serve on juries or hold public office. Once they completed their terms of service, however, they received a grant of land and joined other freeholders as full members of Virginia's body politic.

A *third* class of emigrants received passage from their fellow adventurers. These individuals therefore owed service not to the company but to private persons, some of whom resided in the colony and others of whom resided in England. Since the headright land grants of these individuals were made to their benefactors, they did not automatically become landowning members of the commonwealth upon completion of their indenture. Instead, they remained tenants until they could accumulate enough money to purchase land of their own. Some did. Some never did. Some migrated west. Some returned to England. Others died.

Although opportunity existed for individuals to rise from the lower classes to the higher class, no such trend developed. Instead, the distance separating the classes widened. This was hardly surprising given the colony's agricultural economy. As its headmen accumulated more wealth, their horizons broadened and the opportunities that opened to them expanded in ways that did not for the others. Nor was there room in the commonwealth of Virginia for a bustling corps of merchants to bridge the gap between the first class and the rest of the community.[29] Without tradesmen and shopkeepers to occupy them, towns did not form. Instead, adventurers who had the means followed the practice of the colony's property-owning first class by settling themselves on a parcel of unoccupied land, then expanding their holdings so they could grow more of "the vile stinking weed." Those who could not afford to do this became their servants and lived on their plantations under their control.

The Virginia Company was the colony's largest proprietor. It was also the largest source of demand for labor. Its ongoing efforts to supply its own needs added to the commonwealth's second class of inhabitants. Proprietors of the colony's private plantations (and new adventurers with the financial wherewithal) added steadily to its third class by purchasing the headrights of new arrivals whose passage had been paid by others—often ship captains seeking to profit through the sale of their "cargo."

The forebears of what was to become a fourth class arrived in August of 1619 when one Captain Jope in a Dutch man-of-war bartered twenty Africans for supplies.[30]

The growth that solidified this economic and social stratification also put an end to the notion that the colonists pursed a common good. The proliferation of private plantations after 1616 distributed the population across an increasingly wide and disconnected region. The men who superintended the colony's settlements—commonly the owners of the plantations around which they formed—had *particular* interests, which sharpened as their assets and their appetites grew. Not only did this increase competition for the company's scarce resources, it overburdened the company's always-meager capacity to provide customer services.

Kingsbury referred to "factions which developed and which resulted finally in the dissolution of the company."[31] The conflicts, which defined their interactions, sharpened during the colony's

Landing of Negroes at Jamestown
from a Dutch Man-of-War, 1619

transformation from commune to commonwealth. These centered on the competing interests of the planters who formed the colony's body politic, on the divergent visions of the company's directors, and on the unfilled expectations of its investors. Although the king remained aloof from these conflicts, by 1622 his Privy Council had become a referee in an increasing number of these complaints.

Corruption

Edmund Morgan showed that the conflicts between these factions were aggravated by corruption:

Among the worst offenders were the company's own officials in the colony. In Sandys' shipments of men bound to the company, they had perceived an opportunity for exploiting not only the tenants but the company itself. The fact that the men arrived without adequate provisions furnished an excuse for treating tenants as servants. Instead of being seated on company lands where they were supposed to clear, fence, plant, and build, the tenants were hired out to private planters....Although the officers reported that they hired out the sickly, rather than the able-bodied, the company got word that it was the other way round: the strongest men, who might have benefited the company most, were put to work on private plantations. And "where it is pretended this placing them with old planters is for their health, they are so unmercifully used that it is the greatest cause of our tenants' discontent...." Thus while company men labored on the lands of private planters, company land went uncleared, unfenced, and unplanted.[32]

Planters also found ways to cheat the company. "A magazine," Morgan explained, "was supposed to turn a profit by exchanging supplies for tobacco or other commodities, but it became the practice in Virginia to sell for the promise of tobacco when the next crop was in; and somehow the promises were not kept. The floating taverns got the tobacco before it could reach the cape merchant in charge of the magazine, and all magazines seem to have ended with a loss to the investors in England."[33]

Tobacco formed the hazy center of a broader problem, which Edwin Sandys discussed in his address to the company's court on 11 June 1621: "Touching Tobacco which hath been always so generally affected by the planters in Virginia, Sir Edwin Sandys signified how extremely displeasing it was to the King and scandalous unto the plantation and unto the company, that notwithstanding it [the enterprise] hath been prosecuted these many years by many wise and worthy persons and wasted in that time a mass of money

Jamestown during Sir George Yeardley's Governorship, 1620

yet hath it not produced any other effect, than that smokie weed of Tobacco, and therefore the counsel as heretofore it may appear by all their former instructions and letters, so now again had taken it into their consideration how they might restrain the general planting thereof or at least bring it down to a far less proportion and quantity than now is made."[34]

This complaint was justified on the practical grounds that Virginia's planters were growing tobacco instead of the food crops they needed to feed themselves. But it also reflected the enlightened sentiments that shaded Sandys' vision of the new society that Virginia was supposed to be. "The company was not only interested in the economic and industrial development and the necessary political forms of the colony," Kingsbury explained, referring to Sandys' hopes for his commonwealth, "but as Sir Edwin Sandys declared, it had a higher purpose than the Muscovy or other commercial corporations. . . ."[35] Such an enlightened entity should not have rested on smoke and yet it did. Why? Because tobacco provided the best return to the planters who sustained it. According to the records of the Virginia Company, Sandys "further declared that the chiefest cause that all other commodities were neglected was found to be the long maintaining of the high price of tobacco at 3s the pound, which had already destroyed the magazine of at least 1,000 pound charge unto certain adventurers for apparel and other necessary provisions whereof the colony stood in need; which they repaid in nothing but tobacco forcing it at that price upon the cape merchant whereof a good part of it was scarce sold and now again they have repaid the whole company in the like manner at the same price for all the charge they have been at for sending them apprentices, servants, and wives, which cost the company nearly 2,000 pounds."[36]

Profit versus Principle

The problem that embittered Sandys and his supporters (and the king) was the consequence, in other words, of the very policy they had implemented to attract enterprising individuals. Tobacco was at the center of a conflict between *profit* and *principle*. The losses the company's investors suffered in its tobacco trading (which were caused in part by paying premium prices for stocks of substandard quality) ignited the most destructive of its internal conflicts. While some of the company's larger investors may have viewed these losses as the cost of longer-term profits, smaller investors were increasingly inclined to interpret them as evidence of corruption and mismanagement—and as grounds for legal action.

Despite the company's dismal financial results, it was able to replace the capital it lost for more than a decade. Some of it came from the sale of stock to new adventurers. Some of it came from "special collections and particular gifts for the advancement of religion and of education in the colony." By far the greatest share of the company's new funds came from *lotteries* that King James had licensed the company to conduct in 1612. Kingsbury explained, "That the company depended on the lotteries is indicated by the following statements in court book: On December 1, 1619, the lotteries were continued until summer because there was no other means of securing money, and the plan put forth for the development of the colony on July 7, 1620, provided that the estimated expense of 17,000 pounds should be met by the income from the lotteries, which would amount to 18,000 pounds."[37]

Disaster struck on 8 March 1620 when the king eliminated this critical source of funding with "a proclamation commanding the Virginia Company to forbear license for keeping and continuing any lottery." Kingsbury reported the results this way:

> The overthrow of lotteries carried consternation to the company. An income was essential with which to send out settlers to develop the soil or to create new industries, but the general stock was so low that the company could not even carry out its plan for glassworks. Finally, after several months of discussion, recourse was had to special adventure or new joint stock companies for special undertakings, controlled by a treasurer who should be elected by the adventurers in the scheme. Thus followed the creation of a series of magazines for the erection of a glass furnace, the establishment of a fur trade, for sending maids for wives, and for supplying a magazine for apparel. The records of these ventures are to be found only in the court book, and the data there given is very insufficient. This, of course, meant no advantage to the general stock, and the company was forced to discover means for securing returns from the general investment and an income with which to develop the company's land. Hence, private plantations were organized, and private patents and monopolies for the industry of pitch and tar, for iron works, for new discoveries were granted, while special commissions for trade along the coast and for fishing added to the revenue.[38]

Most of these ventures eventually failed, but since they were separately funded their losses were not borne by the company's investors. This spared the company an additional agony, but it provided no solution to its acute financial problems.

The Indian Uprising of 1622

The company's death knell sounded at midday on 22 March 1622 when the Powhatan Indians launched a coordinated attack on its colonial settlements.[39] The financial consequences were even more devastating than the massacre of 347 of its adventurers[40] as the company was forced to expend nonexistent capital to replenish the colony with supplies and men. The situation continued to deteriorate through the winter of 1623 when food shortages and disease claimed another 500 lives.

In these desperate circumstances, the company's directors began to reconsider their position in respect to tobacco. According to Kingsbury, "the private grants did not promise sufficient income to meet the great demands for supplies for the general stock which the massacre of 1622 brought about. As a result the company turned to the income from tobacco, regardless of its high purposes and its endeavors to enforce the production of other commodities. This feeling of the importance of a contract for the sole importation of tobacco took such a strong hold upon the company that from May, 1622, until its dissolution, just a year later, nothing else worth mentioning is recorded in the court book...."[41]

On 30 December 1619, King James issued a proclamation to restrain the planting of tobacco in England and Wales. On 10 April 1620, the Privy Council issued an order allowing the sole importation of tobacco into England, but to a contractor other than the Virginia Company. In its 5 June 1622 court, Sir Edwin Sandys delivered a piece of news that probably encouraged his unsteady cohorts. The Lord High Treasurer of England, the director of his

The Jamestown Massacre of 1622

Majesty's finances, and by good fortune "one of the most ancient adventurers" in the Virginia Company, after reviewing the contract by which his Majesty supplied his kingdom with tobacco, had offered the company an opportunity to take over the management of this vital business.[42]

The council discussed the matter in its May and June courts and took it up again in its court on 3 July 1622, when "the contract to be made with his Majesty by said companies for the sole importation of tobacco now offered unto them by the Lord High Treasurer of England, concerning which the said committees having consulted long about it, after mature deliberation had thereupon, offered unto the consideration of the Lord Treasurer certain propositions which are entered verbatim in the said court. In answer whereunto his lp: delivered three exceptions unto which the committee had also made reply with an addition of certain causes agreed unto to be inserted in the contract, having been omitted in the first propositions...."[43]

The company objected to the king's demand for an allowance to bring in "60,000 pounds weight of Spanish tobacco or otherwise 40,000 weight to be brought in by some other."[44] It proposed instead to limit such an allowance to two years and 40,000 pounds and that "the markets in Spain be open and free as formerly they have been." Negotiations continued on these and other fine points until at length a bargain was reached by which the company agreed to deliver a third of the tobacco it landed in England to the king under a contract that would run for seven years.

That the council considered this deal risky is suggested by its protracted deliberations. Finally, "after a long pause for so much as it appeared no more could be said than had been formerly delivered, My Lord [Southampton who was then treasurer of the Virginia Company] at length at the request of the Court put the propositions to the question, whither they did agree and fully consent that this contract should go forward." It was to be made with the King and provide him with the right to the sole importation of tobacco into England on the conditions that had been formerly proposed. The council "with one unanimous consent" signified its approval of the "said bargain, by a general erection of hands with contradiction save only one hand held up against it."[45]

Whether this contract would have salvaged the company's finances will never be known because on 28 April 1623 the Privy Council dissolved it. By this time, the company was essentially dysfunctional. Kingsbury described the beleaguered state of its affairs:

"The movement begins in the year just preceding the ascension of Sir Edwin Sandys to the position of treasurer, and seems to have had its origin in the trouble over Sir Samuel Argall and the appointment of Sir George Yeardley as governor of the colony. It finally involved many of the personal complaints and difficulties, which presented themselves to the company....The measures, which thus arose with regard to these individuals are to be found chiefly in the court book....The subjects discussed include such problems as the relations with the northern colony, the conflict with Spain concerning the ship *Treasurer*, the suit against William Wye for failing to land settlers in Virginia, and various accusations against Governor Yeardley and Captain Argall for misgovernment in the colony. The accounts of Sir Thomas Smythe, the settlement of Alderman Robert Johnson's accounts for the magazine, and the illegality of Captain John Martin's patent for a plantation were also questions which were of vital importance to the financial affairs of the company and took the attention of numerous courts...."[46]

Edmund Morgan verified the allegations against Yeardley: "[He] found Virginia a rewarding environment from the beginning. According to John Pory, when Yeardley arrived there in 1610, he carried nothing more valuable than a sword. But when he visited London in 1617, after his first term as governor of Virginia, he was able 'out of his mere gettings here' to spend 'very near three thousand pounds.' Before returning to the colony he got himself knighted, and Londoners observed that 'he flaunted it up and down the streets in extraordinary bravery, with fourteen or fifteen fair liveries after him." Morgan described how Yeardley as governor was assigned three thousand acres and one hundred tenants to cultivate it. But when he finished his term in 1621, he returned only forty-six tenants. Morgan interpreted this behavior noting, "Yeardley, whom William Capp characterized as a 'right worthy statesman, for his own profit,' did not give up his tenants and records contain accusations against him of appropriating servants belonging to other planters and of keeping as a servant a young man whose relatives had paid his way." These practices seemingly allowed Yeardley to become rich even as his company stumbled into insolvency. "At his death," Morgan concluded, "Yeardley's estate was apparently valued at only about 10,000 pounds. But it is not unlikely that he had already transferred much of what he owned to his wife and children in order to circumvent the litigation that a substantial will often produced."[47]

Kingsbury closed the chapter on Edwin Sandys' commonwealth with this postscript:

"The judgment was rendered on the morrow of Holy Trinity, and declares that Nicholas Ferrar and the others are convicted of the usurpation of privileges and that the 'said privileges are taken and seized into the hand of the King and the said Nicholas Ferrar and the others shall not intermeddle but shall be excluded from the usurpation of liberties, privileges, and franchises of the same so taken from the King, and that they are to satisfy to the King his fine for the usurpation of said privileges.' The writ of *quo warranto* was issued out of the Kings Bench on Tuesday next after the morrow of All Saints (November 4, 1623). The suit was opened on the Friday after the quindecim of St. Martin's (November 28), and was then postponed until the eighth of Hillary (January 20). It was postponed a second time to the quindecim of Easter (April 11), and judgment was finally rendered on the morrow of Trinity (May 24, 1624)."[48]

The King's Reclamation

Robert Beverly, the iconoclastic planter who chronicled Virginia's first century in 1704, was pleased by the results, though he was mistaken in giving credit to Charles I. It was actually his father, James I, who dissolved the company. "The fatal consequences of the company's male-administration cried so loud," Beverly erroneously asserted, "that King Charles the first, coming to the Crown of England, had a tender concern for the poor people that had been betrayed thither, and lost. Upon which consideration he dissolved the company in the year 1626, reducing the country and government into his own immediate direction, appointing the governor and council himself, and ordering all patents and process to issue in his own name, reserving only to himself an easy quit-rent of two shillings for every hundred acres of land, and so pro rato."[49]

Morgan agreed with Beverly that the English monarch was justified to repossess his property in Virginia. "Because the Stuart kings became a symbol of arbitrary government," he observed, "and because Sir Edwin Sandys was a champion of Parliamentary power and was even accused at the time of being a republican, historians for long interpreted the dissolution of the Virginia Company as a blow dealt to democracy by tyranny. Modern scholarship has altered the verdict and shown that any responsible monarch would have been obliged to stop the reckless shipment of his subjects to their death."

The concept upon which King James I rested his new royal government was different from the one that Edwin Sandys had implemented in promoting his concept of commonwealth. Sandys had endeavored in a vaguely Lockean way to create a common communal interest by encouraging individuals to build profit-generating businesses to support his company's market. The king operated on the vaguely Hobbesian notion that he served the common good by maintaining *his* kingdom. He sought to do this in his new dominion in the same way he did in England—through a phalanx of powerful lieutenants.

The magnitude of the change James I introduced is obscured by superficial similarities between the government he was instituting and the one he was replacing. Like the old one, the new one had a governor and a council of state. The king even reappointed the man (Francis Wyatt) who had been governor of Virginia at the time of the company's demise. And, on the condition that they swear allegiance to him, James I commissioned ten of Virginia's most prominent men to serve him and to support the governor as councilors of state.

As an instrument of the Virginia Company, the council's responsibility had been to "bend [its] care and endeavors to assist the said governor; first and principally, in the advancement of the honor and service of God, and the enlargement of his kingdom, amongst the heathen people; and next, in erecting of the said colony in due obedience to his Majesty, and all lawful authority from his Majesty's directions; and lastly in maintaining the people in Justice and Christian conversation amongst themselves, and in strength and ability to withstand their enemies." The council had similar responsibilities under the new royal government, "ordering, managing and governing of the affairs of that colony and plantation and of the persons there already inhabiting or which hereafter shall be or inhabit there until some other constant and settled course be resolved and established by us [James I]."[50]

But where Sandys' commonwealth required mechanisms to define the common good and to implement laws that promoted them, the kingdom of James I required only that the king's subjects be obedient to the will of their sovereign. The new royal colony therefore did not need, or have, a General Assembly. Without a forum in which to cultivate a common communal interest, the commonwealth became moribund.

James I assumed that he could command the obedience of his subjects without being a tyrant. As if to prove it, he endorsed a policy similar to Sandys', declaring "the said colony should have diverse lands, grounds, havens, ports, commodities, hereditaments and diverse privileges and liberties for the quiet settling and good government in the said plantations." He wanted his subjects, in other words, to continue to generate business profits. Now, however, the purpose was to enhance *his Majesty's* financial well-being. The interests of his colonial subjects were now subservient to this larger end.

James I disbanded the colonial legislature to suppress development of a rival will. His new government was, however, no less vulnerable in this respect. While the governor was arguably the king's man, his council was filled with men who were deft at promoting their own interests. Indeed, they were valuable to the king because they had wealth and influence. He elevated them in order to help himself. But in doing so, he placed them in positions where they could help themselves—which they did. The new colonial government was therefore a breeding ground for political conflict. The king's man by turns cajoled and threatened his councilors to tow his Majesty's line. The headmen who comprised his council, when not resisting these pressures, pressed their own interests. Only on the perimeter of this sharpening rivalry was there room for concern about *the people*. Within a mere generation, this pattern solidified into a tradition. The large planters who filled the council of state emerged as the *Tidewater oligarchy*. Their domination of the colony's government and society would continue for 150 years.

As a body politic, Virginia's political establishment was not quite Lockean because it excluded the great majority of the population. By Lockean standards, its government was not quite tyrannical because the power it exercised was within its right. The mutinies its members periodically raised to gain and defend their political power were neither Lockean rebellions nor Lockean revolutions because the general population was never involved and the "legislative" was never reconstituted.

Charles I succeeded his father on 5 March 1625. In an attempt to resurrect itself, the assembly sent the new king a petition requesting that he endorse its continuation. Charles I denied the petition. Instead, as Wilcomb Washburn reported, he "assured the planters that though the form of Virginia's government had changed, the individual planters could be sure that their rights and property would be respected. Charles informed the colonists, however, that he would take over the buying of their tobacco as a royal monopoly and give them such prices as would satisfy and encourage them." Washburn continued by noting that, "agreement with the planters, nevertheless, was difficult to obtain. The Virginians were solidly united as a special interest in favoring the highest prices and the greatest production. Their representatives in the House of Burgesses and on the Virginia Council, were their ardent spokesmen, themselves planters, whose interest lay in fighting the battle of all Virginians."[51]

Charles I, King of England (1600–1649)

Tobacco-growing Virginians may have been unified in their desire to get "the highest prices and the greatest production," but Washburn's assertion that their unity was "solid" is belied by his own words: "[A]lthough the King made no specific provision for the continuation of a representative Assembly, Wyatt and the Council called together representatives of various settlements to meet in a General Assembly on May 10, 1625, in Jamestown. There they drew up a petition complaining of the old Company rule and the miserable state in which it had kept the colony during the previous twelve years, and pleading with the King not to allow a monopoly of the tobacco trade. The King's advisors, they feared, were those who had formerly oppressed them and who would do so again should the King consent to a 'pernicious contract' taking all their tobacco at unfair rates."[52]

That the governor would call this assembly indicates that the support of the colony's leading planters was important to his administration. The king himself soon realized this. Washburn explained:

> Meanwhile the King had grown increasingly disgusted that Virginia's economy continued to be "built on smoke," and he ordered the Virginians to concentrate on crops and products other than tobacco.... Charles directed that a general assembly of planters be summoned to deal with his proposals, and Governor West and the Council ordered an Assembly to meet on March 10, 1628. The Assembly thanked the King for prohibiting the importation of Spanish tobacco into the English market, but cried that they would be at the mercy of covetous individuals in England if a monopoly on Virginia tobacco were allowed. They proposed, however, that since the King intended to take all their tobacco, he should agree to take at least 500,000 pounds of tobacco at 3 shillings 6 pence the pound delivered in Virginia, or 4 shillings delivered in London. If the King was unwilling to take so much, they desired the right to export again from England to the Low Countries, Ireland, Turkey, and elsewhere.[53]

FIVE

The Rule Under Law of Gentlemen

Charles I, King of England had no need for a general assembly in Virginia. It was clear enough to His Royal Majesty that the good the colony served was to promote *his* royal interests. He therefore abolished the colonial parliament upon his ascension to the throne in 1625. This placed his governors in a difficult position since it was it was all but impossible to accomplish His Majesty's purposes without the cooperation of the colony's leading men. Charles finally consented to reconstitute the assembly (1642). Seven years after this "gratious" gesture, he was condemned to death and beheaded by the parliamentarians who had defeated him in England's Civil War. Preoccupied with the construction of a new society in England, Parliament had little time to manage affairs in Virginia. And so the government of the colony passed for the first time into the hands of Virginians. Elevated by their new authority, her leading planters became in effect a *governing class*. They were quick to exercise their power by promoting the sale of their tobacco into a world market. Not until later did the legislature follow England's republican Parliament in using its power over the purse to subjugate the colony's executive.

I T TOOK NEARLY THIRTY YEARS for a civil society to form in Virginia. During the next eighty years, the colony's leading citizens consolidated the power of its government in their own hands. They did this with several minor mutinies and a few notable palace coups. In certain notable instances the rebellions were against members of their own class.

The proposals and counter-proposals that constituted James I's interactions with the governor's council confirm that by 1627 Virginia's headmen had formed a political will of their own. Morgan suggested that it existed in 1624: "They had already experienced the power that distance gave them in circumventing the order sent by the Virginia Company. And even before the king took control of Virginia's government, they took steps to secure their position. Meeting in the last assembly under the company, the governor's council and the House of Burgesses affirmed that the governor (who would henceforth be appointed by the king) should have no power to levy taxes without the consent of the assembly."[54]

Morgan explained evidence of an underlying a political will this way:

Between the lines the assemblymen were saying that Virginians would find ways of defeating any English policy toward them that they did not approve. And they soon showed that they could defeat projects sponsored by the king as easily as those sponsored by the company. Although Charles pointedly refrained from continuing the assembly when he took over the government of Virginia, royal governors found that they could not get along without it or without the council. Actually, the council had been officially continued, and to it the king, like the company appointed the most successful and powerful men in the colony. As the number of such men grew, however, they could not all be given places on the council, and yet it was necessary to take them into account. The assembly offered the easiest way to do it. Though without instructions to do so, governors called the assembly together on several occasions in the 1620s and 1630s to deal with problems of defense and other matters.[55]

Wesley Frank Craven suggested that if the king had been less concerned with monopolizing Virginia's tobacco trade and diversifying its economy, he might have been able to govern his colony without calling the planters into assembly. Driven as he was by his own economic interests (and other high purposes) he had little choice but to deal with the colony's headmen. But contrary to his purpose, his efforts succeeded only in empowering a political establishment with a competing will. While this establishment was sinking its roots, Robert Beverly explained, "people flocked over thither apace; everyone took up Land by Patent to his Liking; and not minding any thing but to be Masters of great Tracts of Land, they planted themselves separately on their several Plantations....This Liberty of taking up Land, and the Ambition each Man had of being Lord of a vast, tho' unimproved Territory, together with the Advantage of the many Rivers, which afforded a commodious Road for Shipping at every Man's Door, has made the Country fall into such an unhappy Settlement and Course of Trade; that to this Day they have not any one Place of Cohabitation among them, that may reasonably bear the Name of a Town."[56]

This was the attitude and situation of *the people* of Virginia when Governor Yeardley died in November 1627. The council selected one of its members, Captain Francis West, to take his seat pending the king's appointment of a new governor.

Charles named Captain John Harvey to the post on 26 March 1628. Harvey headed the commission that had investigated the state of colonial affairs prior to the establishment of the new royal government in 1625 and was therefore in the king's favor and known to his subjects in Virginia. When a year passed and Harvey did not arrive, the council elected the notorious Dr. John Pott to succeed Francis West as acting governor.

Washburn described Pott's character in these words: "Few men possess a less savory record than this first representative of the medical profession in America. In 1624 he had been ordered removed from the Virginia Council, at the insistence of the Earl of Warwick, for his part in the attempt to poison the colony's Indian foes. He was later convicted of cattle stealing but spared punishment because he was the only doctor in the colony and therefore in great demand." According to Washburn, "Both Pott and West had been foes of the Indians, and in numerous orders and proclamations denounced former treaties of peace with them, and directed that perpetual enmity and wars be maintained against them. A pretended peace was, however, authorized to be extended to the Indians in August 1628 until certain captive Englishmen were redeemed; then it was to be broken."[57]

Harvey arrived in time to prevent this war. In its stead, he implemented an earlier plan to secure the peninsula between the James and the York rivers with a palisade that would extend from College Creek on its south end to Queen's Creek on its north end. Harvey would also enlist the cooperation of the council to revise the colony's laws and to organize it into counties where monthly courts could be administered by local justices of the peace. This cooperative effort bore additional fruit: the production of formerly neglected food crops increased to a level where the colony was able to feed itself.

The Harvey Affair

Despite these accomplishments, the goodwill between Harvey and the headmen of Virginia did not last long. "The causes of the revolt against Harvey were various," Washburn reported. "Of first importance was the continual opposition that existed between the Governor and his Council. The revolt was not primarily a revolt of the people but a revolt by certain members of the Council who attempted to give their particular subordination the appearance of a general rebellion." [58]

Beverly pinpointed the real source of the problem in describing the founding of the colony of Maryland by Cacilius Calvert, Lord Baltimore, who was a Roman Catholic:

His Lordship finding all Things in this Discovery according to his Wish returned to England. And because the Virginia settlements at that time reached no further than the South Side of the Potomac River, his Lordship got a grant of the propriety of Maryland, bounding it to the south by Potomac River, on the Western Shore, and by an East Line from Point Look-out, on the Eastern Shore; But died himself before he could embark for the promised land.... By this unhappy accident a country which Nature had so well contrived for one, became two separate governments. This produced a most unhappy inconvenience to both; for these two being the only countries under the Dominion of England, that plant tobacco in any quantity, the consequence of that division is, that when one colony goes about to prohibit the trash of that commodity, to help the market, then the other, to take advantage of that market, pours into England all they can make, both good and bad, without distinction.[59]

The unwelcome prospect of competition was quite likely overshadowed by resentment. The land-hungry planters who comprised Virginia's political and social establishment had their own plans for the vast and fertile tract across the Potomac. His Lordship's coup was therefore more than opportunity lost. It was an affront to their propriety. Beverly described additional fallout: "Neither was this all the mischief that happened to poor Virginia upon this grant; for the example had dreadful consequences, and was in the end one of the occasions of another massacre by the Indians. For this precedent of my Lord Baltimore's grant, which was hint enough for other courtiers, (who never intended a settlement, as my Lord did) to find out something of the same kind to make money of. This was the occasion of several very large defalcations from Virginia within

George Calvert, 1st Lord Baltimore (1580–1632)

a few years afterwards; which were forwarded and assisted by the contrivance of the Governor Sir John Harvey."[60]

This transgression caused the men of Virginia's governing class to find Harvey's other faults intolerable. "As this gentleman was irregular in this," Beverly reported, "so he was very unjust and arbitrary in his other methods of government. He improved fines and penalties, which the unwary assemblies of those times had given chiefly to him. He was so haughty and furious to the Council, and to the best gentlemen of the country, that his tyranny grew at last unsupportable." And so, in the year 1639, the council sent him back to London, a prisoner in the company of two of its members who would press the charges against him. As might be expected, upon news of his arrival, Charles I was angered. Without hearing anything more, he reinstated Harvey as governor.

Charles I had close ties to the Roman Church through his wife Henrietta Maria, daughter of the French king, and through his grandmother, Mary Queen of Scots. The king inadvertently precipitated Harvey's problems by instructing him to aid Baltimore's effort to establish his colony in Maryland. In the face of this unexpected crisis, Charles I was forced to make a choice. In the end, he chose not to cross the council. Beverly abbreviated this story in reporting, "by the next shipping he was graciously pleased to change him [Harvey]; and so made amends for this man's male-administration, by sending in the good and just Sir William Berkeley to succeed him."[61]

Not until 11 January 1639 did the king actually replace Harvey. On that day, he appointed Sir Francis Wyatt to serve yet another term as governor of Virginia. Wyatt held the post until Berkeley arrived in March of 1642. In the meantime, to erase any residue of hard feelings among the lords of his province, Charles I authorized the reestablishment of their assembly.

The "tyranny" that triggered this, the first of several mutinies raised by Virginia's governing class, had little to do with the oppression of *the people* of the colony and nothing at all to do with the representation that the large majority of them entirely lacked. Nor had the king exercised power beyond his right in helping his Catholic subject settle a territory that the Virginians never managed to invade. This episode in the continuing contest for political power was therefore neither a Lockean *revolution* nor a Lockean *rebellion*. It stands today as the occasion in which the Tidewater oligarchy first asserted its sovereignty. It would be a precedent for its next exercise of its sovereign authority, which occurred sixteen years later.

Berkeley's Bluster

Professor Warren M. Billings gave this introduction to the storied governor of Virginia:

Service in the First and Second Bishops' Wars (1639–1640) won Berkeley a knighthood as it disillusioned him about the wisdom of the king's policies that provoked the Scots to rebellion and edged his fellow Englishmen nearer the brink of civil war. About the

Sir William Berkeley, Governor of Virginia
(1642–1652 / 1661–1677)

time of the execution of Thomas Wentworth, 1st earl of Strafford, Berkeley concluded that his time at court was drawing to an end, so he turned elsewhere for preferment. For a brief while he toyed with the idea of taking up residence at Istanbul, but abruptly he changed direction. Virginia, he decided, was the more inviting prospect. He used his relations and friends to engineer his purchase of the office of governor from the incumbent, and in August 1641 Charles commissioned him to succeed Sir Francis Wyatt. The position set him on a personal transformation not at all unlike that experienced by other English immigrants who went out to the colony in search of aggrandizement....[62] (emphasis added)

Berkeley's story was interrupted by the English civil war in which the forces of Parliament battled against those loyal to the king. The Parliamentary side was to win this contest. After passing through a brief period of republican government, the new model collapsed and the monarchy was restored.

The civil war in England became a political crisis in Virginia two years after Parliament beheaded England's king on 30 January 1649. Governor Berkeley precipitated this crisis in the course of condemning Parliament's "tyrannical and bloody" actions. "But gentlemen," Berkeley announced at the conclusion of his oration, "by the grace of God we will not so tamely part with our King, and all these blessings we enjoy under him; and if they oppose us, do but follow me, I will either lead you to victory or loose a life which I cannot more gloriously sacrifice then to my loyalty, and your security."[63]

This lofty pronouncement of fealty overshadowed a more practical consideration. On 3 October 1650, Parliament enacted a measure it had been considering for more than three years.[64] Finally able to focus on business after the dispatch of their ungovernable king, Parliament had passed its first Navigation Act. By requiring that all colonial goods be carried in English ships, it effectively banished Dutch merchants from Virginia's ports. Such a prohibition materially diminished the economic prospects of Virginia's planters because Dutch merchants paid higher prices for their tobacco than did the English.

Governor Berkeley's royalist blustering notwithstanding, *the people* who "rouzed themselves" against Parliament were the headmen who filled Virginia's General Assembly. Outraged that Parliament would meddle with their markets, they proclaimed, "We are resolved to Continue our Allegiance to our most Gracious King, yet as long as his gracious favor permits us, *we will peaceably (as formerly) trade with the Londoners, and all other Nations* in amity with our Sovereign...."[65] (emphasis added)

Parliament responded with ophidian coolness, sending a fleet to conquer the impudent colony. This armada reached Virginia in January of 1652. Beverly reported, "the Country at first held out vigorously against him [Capt. Dennis, the commander of the English fleet], with Sir William Berkeley, by the assistance of such Dutch vessels as were then there, made a brave resistance. But at last Dennis contrived a stratagem, which betrayed the country. He had got a considerable parcel of goods aboard, which belonged to two of the council; and found a method of informing them of it. By this means they were reduced to the dilemma either of submitting, or losing their goods."[66] What choice did they have? Helpless in the face of

Charles the King Walked for the last time through the streets of London, 1649

this treachery, they capitulated. "This occasioned factions among them; so that at last, after the surrender of all the other English plantations, Sir William was forced to submit to the usurper on the terms of a general pardon."

That Berkeley's bluster worked can be seen in the articles of surrender, which were signed on 12 March 1652.[67] A month later, the commissioners who negotiated this surrender for Parliament

*Sir William Berkeley Surrenders Virginia to the Commissioners
of the Commonwealth, 1652*

called a meeting of the burgesses for the purpose of drawing a plan
under which to govern the colony until a formal instrument could
be developed in England. "This House of Burgesses and the Commissioners acting with them formed a kind of constitutional convention, and their work, owing to the peculiar situation of affairs
existing in England, was allowed to stand, with little interference,
till the close of the common wealth period. According to the framework drawn up, the *Burgesses* were to be the *seat of power*, electing
both the governor and the members of the Council, who were to
assist the governor in executive and judicial matters. The Assembly
at the start consisted of the members of the House of Burgesses and
the Parliamentary Commissioners and then, after the governor and
members of the Council had been elected, of these in addition. It
seems to have been unicameral throughout."[68] (emphasis added)
For the first time, the governor would be drawn from the same pool
as the burgesses and the council.

69

The terms of the surrender called for Berkeley to vacate his office and leave the colony. Berkeley did vacate his post and was replaced in succession by Richard Bennett (1652–1655), Edward Digges (1655–1656), and Samuel Mathews (1656–1660). But instead of leaving the colony, he retired to his Green Springs estate in James City County where he remained until the burgesses recalled him following the sudden death of Governor Mathews.

Shortly after his recall, Berkeley journeyed to England in the hope of gaining financial support for his plan to develop the colony. He undertook this mission it seems without knowing that England's new king was formulating a plan of his own to accomplish this critical objective. "Charles II favored the idea of agricultural diversification and its promise of reducing tobacco production," Billings observed, "but he withheld financial support and flatly turned aside Berkeley's arguments in favor of free trade. Ordered back to his government, Berkeley set sail for Virginia in September 1662, resolutely committed to diversify the colonial economy, but in his own way. That determination was one in a series of missteps that finally ruined him." Billings explained that "Berkeley's economic visions failed because he never accepted Stuart colonial policy, especially the navigation system which was designed to regulate trade between England and her colonies, and he chose to ignore as much of it as possible."[69]

The Burgesses' Coup d'etat

The "constitutional convention" of 1652 conveyed to the gentry of Virginia's Tidewater all of the political power in the colony. They would reign in virtual autonomy for the next eight years. Under the colony's surrender agreement, it was free to trade with every nation. And so, during the commonwealth period, Virginians ignored the Navigation Act of 1650 and traded with the Dutch and whomever else they pleased. The Tidewater's oligarchy was therefore able to establish itself in a period of general prosperity. Sharing power, however, proved difficult even for these like-minded oligarchs.

Victories won by Parliament's new model army at Naseby and Langport in the summer of 1645 decided England's civil war in favor of the Parliamentary side. The ensuing exodus of defeated (and dispossessed) royalists brought many families whose names are now an essential part of Virginia history. The Carters, Lees, Randolphs, and Byrds were joined by the Harrisons, Pages, Wormleys, and Burwells, and by the Masons, Beverleys, Carys, Nelsons, Ludwells, and Fitzhughs. The influx of these "men of quality" deepened the patrician character of Virginia's planter society, which was soon to be reflected in the colony's government.

The new assembly convened on 25 November 1652. Over the next five years, it would follow the pattern established in this inaugural session. Administrative matters constituted its first order of business. Having disposed of these, the burgesses would settle disputes and petitions pertaining to land ownership. When this work was completed, they would create business opportunities for themselves and their constituents in the name of the common good.[70]

In its meeting on 25 March 1658, the assembly deliberated on a sensitive new matter. In an effort to streamline and simplify its work, it proposed that "all propositions and laws exhibited" by the committee of public affairs first be "treated on in the House by the Burgesses in private or in presence of the Governor and Council." The burgesses then resolved "by a general consent that they shall be first discussed among the Burgesses only."[71] This undoubtedly offended their haughty peers in the executive branch. Perhaps to assuage these hard feelings, the assembly resolved five days later to institute a poll tax to fund a new stipend for the governor.[72]

Whatever goodwill the burgesses engendered with the governor they probably squandered with his councilors when on 31 March 1658 they enacted measures stating that no portion of the tax be given to the councilors and that each county could continue electing as many burgesses desired:

Proposed, Whether any thing shall be allowed the councilors for their accommodation or not.

Resolved by the first vote nothing to be allowed them.

Proposed, If the Burgesses charge is paid out of the public levy on the tobacco exported, whether it be not necessary to restrain the counties to the election of only two out of a county.

Resolved by the first vote, that there shall be allowed to each county the freedom to elect as many Burgesses as formerly....

This day all the former acts having been perused by the committee for viewing and regulating them were by the said committee presented to the house, where being read and seriously discussed they were approved of in the House and a committee appointed to present them to the Governor and Council, and to advise with him and his council about the explanation or alteration of any seeming difficulties or inconveniences. *Yet with this limitation not to assent to any thing of consequence without the approbation of the House.*[73] (emphasis added)

The meaning of these transactions was no doubt clear to the governor and his men on the council. But if there was a question, the burgesses confirmed their power-gathering ambitions in declaring that nothing be decided without their official approval. They clearly saw themselves as the most powerful players.

Governor Mathews responded by dissolving the assembly. The burgesses showed their mettle the following day. Invoking the same authority that produced the so-called Long Parliament in England (1640–1648), they declared:

That we have in our selves the full power of the election and appointment of all officers in this country until such time as we shall have order to the contrary from the supreme power in England. . . And for the better manifestation thereof and the present dispatch of the affairs of this country we declare as follows:

That wee are not dissolvable by any power yet extant in Virginia but our own, that all former election of Governor and Council be void and null; that the power of governor for the future shall be conferred on Col. Samuel Mathews, Esq. who by us shall be invested with all the just rights and privileges belonging to the Governor and Capt. General of Virginia and that a council shall be nominated, appointed and confirmed, by the present burgesses convened (with the advice of the Governor, for his assistance,) And that for the future none be admitted a councilor but such who shall be nominated, appointed and confirmed by the house of Burgesses as aforesaid, until further order from the supreme power in England.[74]

Washburn summarized the state of affairs after this storm had blown over. "The Assembly of 1659 marks the high water point of local government in Virginia. Not only were the Burgesses supreme in matters of general legislation, compelling the Governor and Secretary to bow to their sovereign power, but in their home counties affairs were conducted much as the local justices saw fit."[75] Washburn might have added that the power these men wielded belonged to the class from which they all came. Even though they shared membership in the same closed society, when they had the opportunity to exercise political power, they maneuvered in ways that divided them against themselves.

Billings added this note to this important chapter in the history of *government by the people*:

The sudden death of Governor Samuel Mathews, Jr. in January 1660 opened the door to Berkeley's own restoration that March. Resuming his former place, Sir William chose to continue his designs for Virginia, which Cromwell had interrupted. Now, however, he realized they could not work without two prerequisites. First, and foremost, he needed the blessing and financial backing of Charles II. Then he had to sell his ideas to the planters at large.... Confident of his talents for persuasion and the logic of his arguments, Berkeley went back to England in 1661 to mount his campaign for royal support. His brother and his friends assured him a ready hearing at court, and so, he discovered, did his seat on the *newly-created Council for Foreign Plantations*. He lobbied publicly and privately for almost a year. The set piece in the effort was his *Discourse and View of Virginia*, which put forth his prescriptions for Virginia's improvements. He achieved something less than he intended. While the king affirmed the concept of diversification, he refused his financial support. Charles likewise warmed to the possibility of limiting tobacco, and he instructed Berkeley to negotiate an agreement with the government of Maryland. More critically, he rejected Berkeley's plea for free trade, but he encouraged the building of more towns throughout the colony.[76] (emphasis added)

The English Commonwealth and Protectorate

The people's government, which ruled England during this period, had similar power struggles. What is known today as the Long Parliament began in 1640 following the so-called Bishops' Wars. Having unceremoniously dissolved Parliament the previous year, bankrupt Charles I summoned the body in desperation after the defeat of his army by the Scots. He hoped to win passage of bills that would allow him to renew his military offensive. He got nothing he wished and everything he likely feared. Under the leadership of John Pym, Parliament enacted a legislative program that deprived Charles I of the power of absolute rule. It disbanded his Star Chamber court, forced him to acknowledge that only the members of the Parliament could dissolve their assembly, and stated that the King was obliged to call them into session at least once every three years.

What is remembered today as the Rump Parliament was constituted of the members who remained from this Long Parliament after what is called "Pride's Purge" in 1648. Colonel Thomas Pride's regiment was involved in the military occupation of London following Charles I's escape from confinement and his failed attempt to form an alliance with the Scots. Under Pride's direction, Presbyterians and Royalists who were thought to be negotiating an agreement with the king were prevented from taking their seats in the House of Commons. This abbreviated body, called Rump Parliament, then ordered the trial of Charles I, condemned him to death, and presided over his execution on 30 January 1649. On 19 May, the Rump Parliament passed *An Act Declaring England to be a Commonwealth* in which it abolished the monarchy and the House of Lords. In this same measure it declared that "the Representatives of the People in Parliament and by such as they shall appoint and constitute as Officers and Ministers under them for the good of the People" would henceforth be the supreme authority in the commonwealth. Having executed the king and abolished the monarchy, Parliament confiscated the lands of the Crown and the Church and sold them to raise needed funds.

Oliver Cromwell returned to England from his successful war against the King of Spain in the spring of 1653. He decided soon after his return that this Rump Parliament was not following a course that suited him.[77] Objecting to its methods and its measures, and noting that it no longer had the support of the army, he replaced it with [140] members nominated entirely by himself. This would be known as the Nominated or Barebones Parliament, its name coming from one Praise-God Barebones, a representative from London. Fearing the political disruption from radical groups, such as Diggers and the Fifth Monarchy, the more moderate Levelers, who controlled this Parliament, voted its dissolution on 12 December 1653.

The dissolution of the Barebones Parliament effectively ended the so-called English commonwealth. It was replaced by the *Protectorate* of Oliver Cromwell. He governed as a military dictator until his death on 3 September 1658. His government was established under what might be described as a written constitution.

Oliver Cromwell, "Warts and All" (1599–1658)

This *Instrument of Government* was prepared by a group of his military officers. Although this plan called for a Council of State and a Parliament in one house, its power was centered in the executive whose authority was sustained by the army. Parliament thus met during the Protectorate, but exercised no power. In its *Humble Petition and Advice* of 1657, Parliament offered Cromwell the throne, which he rejected. Instead he accepted investment as Lord Protector while seated on the throne of the former king at Westminster Abbey. With this elevation he was given power to appoint members of an upper house and to name his successor.

Cromwell's death triggered a split in the factions that comprised his government. When the army and Parliament failed to agree on how England should be ruled, General George Monck, commander of the English forces in Scotland, marched on London. Upon arriving in the capital, Monck reinstated the House of Lords and the Parliament of 1640. Senior Bishops resumed their seats in the new House of Lords. The final act of Parliament under the Protectorate was to vote its dissolution, which it did on 3 March 1660. New elections in April seated what is known as the *Convention Parliament*. This body, which was dominated by royalists, invited Charles II to return. Accepting this invitation, he entered London on 29 May, his birthday.

Restoration

Among the first acts of the new Parliament was the repeal of the Triennial Act of 1641, which required the king to call Parliament at least every three years. Under the Act of Indemnity and Oblivion, the confiscated lands of the Crown and the Church were restored. In an attempt to improve the balance of English trade and protect English merchants from competition, Parliament passed the *second Navigation Act*, which required that all enumerated articles, including tobacco, be shipped directly to England in vessels owned and manned by Englishmen. This act further required that imports into the colonies be carried in English ships from English ports.

The royalist Parliament also voted the new king an annual revenue of 1,200,000 pounds. This sum, Antonia Fraser reported, "although seemingly adequate, proved difficult to collect and in any case the yield had been over-estimated." Fraser suggested that the king's annual expenses excluding the cost of the wars he waged may have been as high as 1,500,000 pounds. Against these expenses, he had a combined revenue of less than 1,000,000 pounds.[78] Therefore, despite his sizeable allowance, the king was strapped. "The want of money puts all things out of order," Pepys told his diary.[79] It is not surprising under these circumstances that Charles II would look upon his colony in Virginia as a source of revenue. By the time of his coronation on 23 April 1661, he had arranged a special duty on tobacco to be paid to himself.

"King, Parliament, and the financial entrepreneurs of Restoration London co-operated," Louis Rubin explained, "in a system

The Restoration: Charles II Lands at Dover, 1660

designed to funnel the wealth of the colonies through the counting houses of London, enhance the power of the British merchant marine, break the dependence of England upon other countries for raw materials and agricultural products, develop a market for its manufactures, and enable England, rather than the Dutch, to serve as the entrepot through which the produce of the New World would reach Europe. For Virginians it meant that tobacco, their principal export crop, could be placed on sale only in England, and the price that London merchants were willing to pay them was what they would receive."[80]

The royal levies and the sharp decline in tobacco prices caused by the closing of the European market pushed the economy of Virginia into a depression that continued through the Restoration period. Virginia's large planters responded to these destructive measures with a radical new policy of their own. To bring their production costs into line with depressed market prices, they established a perpetually low-cost labor supply. That is, in 1661, Virginia's General Assembly legalized African slavery. This allowed planters with access to credit to purchase a workforce with which they could produce tobacco profitably even at the distressed prices that prevailed through the 1660s and 1670s. Smaller planters, who lacked both a sufficiency of land and the financial resources to buy an African workforce, faced financial ruin. The economic hardships that accompanied the restoration of the English monarchy in this way solidified the stratification of Virginia's social classes on the scale of private wealth. Now, however, its hierarchical system rested on the backs of African slaves. Thus, despite chronically low prices and a perennially weak economy, tobacco production continued to expand through Charles II's reign.[81] Revenues to the king and Parliament rose with the volume of production regardless of the price of Virginia's tobacco.[82]

Land Tenure

The land tenure system upon which Virginia's social hierarchy eventually came to rest traces back to the land grants made after Charles I reclaimed his colony from the Virginia Company in 1624. From that time forward, newly arriving settlers who paid their own passage or the passage of others received grants of the *king's* land. Individuals who received these grants held their lands on the conditions that they improve them *and* pay the king an annual land tax known as a *quitrent*. This tax was assessed in the amount of one shilling for every fifty acres and was payable in tobacco at the rate of one penny per pound. The king therefore had a significant financial interest in the ongoing settlement of Virginia. But because the colony's records were not well maintained, it was never certain who owed the King what. Indeed, planters made deliberate efforts to obscure their ownership of land. The tax base was therefore under-reported; and because of this, taxes due were under-assessed. That these revenues were difficult to collect is confirmed by Virginia's royal governors who regularly referenced large arrears in their reports to their superiors in the Board of Trade. These problems of administration, in a sense, disappeared during Commonwealth/Protectorate because the Parliament left the colony to fend for itself.

The matter took on a different complexion on 18 September 1649 when Charles II, in exile in France, rewarded seven of his loyal followers[83] with a proprietary grant of a territory in Virginia bounded by the Rappahannock River on the south, by the Potomac River on the north, and by the "first heads or springs" of these two rivers on the west.

At the time the grant was made, no one knew where its western boundary lay. The issue remained moot from the date of the grant (18 September 1649) until Charles II regained his throne in 1661. The grant then became active, and the surviving holders[84] of the "Northern Neck Proprietary" held their New World domain with all the rights and privileges of barons in the king's court. This meant they could make their own land grants and levy their own duties on the granted lands.

The Reign of Charles II

Outraged by the execution of his king, Governor Sir William Berkeley organized his colony to resist the authority that had perpetrated the heinous act. This rebellion soon failed leaving Berkeley to face the retribution of England's new *Commonwealth.* Surprisingly, its commissioners offered him generous terms—he was removed from his post, but allowed to retire to his estate at Green Springs. Eight years later, on the eve of the Restoration, the legislature recalled him. Again the colony's chief executive, Berkeley set about reestablishing the preeminence of his office. He did this by packing the legislature and doling out patronage to loyal supporters. Members now of an inner circle, Virginia's governing class acquired a social pedigree to match its accumulating power and wealth. The Restoration and the coronation of Charles II proved to be opening events in a fateful series that led first to Sir William's ruin and then to Colonel Richard Lee's puzzling self-submission. This series followed on parallel tracks, one laid by Sir William in Virginia, the other by Charles' brother, James Duke of York. The two engineers shared the common objective of re-channeling the wealth of the thriving colony. Notable among Berkeley's entourage were Nathaniel Bacon and the marauding bands of Indians he proposed to pacify. James' plan was the more ingenious of the two and involved a more practiced cast of players. Notable among these were the Earl of Shaftesbury; Thomas, 2nd Lord Culpeper; and Thomas, 5th Lord Fairfax.

HE SUBJECTS OF LAND LAW and land grants took on new dimensions when Charles II finally gained his throne in 1661. During the first years of Charles' reign, his brother James, Duke of York, superintended the construction of a colonial policy in which the king's New World plantations were organized into a system of proprietary grants held by his wealthiest lords. Tax policies on these colonial plantations and the revenues they generated were administered by a panel filled with Charles' trusted advisors.

Charles' father had established the precedent for the system of land grants that formed the core of Charles II's colonial policy. It was James, however, who transformed these instruments into building blocks in a grand geopolitical strategy. The men who developed and superintended this strategy were *Tories*—kinsmen and political descendents of the men who had promoted the power of the executive prior to the revolution. These new men typically had personal connections to James and supported his plan to reestablish the authority of the Crown. "The policy which they applied to the colonies," Herbert L. Osgood observed, "was of the same general character as that which they supported at home. For their prominence and influence in colonial affairs they are comparable with Raleigh, Gilbert and their associates in the Elizabethan age and with Gorges, Smith, Sandys, and other colonizers of the early Stuart reigns."[85]

Among the first items of business taken up by the new royal government was creating mechanisms to accomplish this policy. On 4 July 1660, a month after the king's return to England, the Privy Council formed a committee to review petitions from merchants doing business in the colonies.

"Among the members of this body," Osgood reported, "were the lord chamberlain (Earl of Manchester), the lord treasurer (Earl of Southhampton), Lord Say and Sele, Denzill, Hollis, Secretaries, Nicholas and Morrice, and Anthony Ashley Cooper [subsequently the Earl of Shaftesbury]. References appear to this group during the next few months under the name of the committee for foreign plantations or for plantations in America."

"After the Restoration," Osgood continued, "the domestic and foreign trade of England was, so far as possible, administered separately from the trade and other affairs of the plantations. The plantations were treated as a group or unit by themselves. Still, all English interests, however distant in location or in character, were superintended by the leading ministers and privy councilors, aided by such experts as they called to their assistance. Therefore, all interests and policies came to a common clearing-house in the end, and there was a similarity of procedure among all bodies concerned."[86] In fact, the same men presided over the king's colonies in two such clearinghouses. The Council of Trade was established on 7 November 1660. The Council of Foreign Plantations was created on 1 December 1660. The two entities would be combined on 16 September 1672 into the Board of Trade and Plantations, which Anthony Ashley Cooper would direct until 1677.

The men who formed these panels constituted the same sort of political association that had filled Sandys' General Assembly in Virginia. As it was with the men who sat in Virginia's first legislature, there was no clear distinction in the minds of Charles' councilors between promoting the policy of the new royal government and pursuing their own private interests. The policy they implemented was, generally speaking, to administer the kingdom in ways that maximized the king's revenues. The Tories who filled his councils implemented this policy by first taking personal possession of his colonial territories, and then growing them in ways that enriched themselves. The king's revenues grew then on their margins.

Charles I had established the Stuarts' first New World proprietary with his grant to Lord Calvert. Charles II followed it fifteen years later by granting the first Lord Culpeper and his fellow retainers a tract of land on the northern rim of Virginia. Two years after his coronation Charles II made another such grant, this one to Lord Shaftesbury and seven of his associates for a vast tract of land that bordered Virginia on the south. After seizing the Dutch colony of New Netherlands in May of 1664, Charles II gifted this territory to his brother. James in turn granted the region bounded by the Hudson and the Delaware rivers to his friends Sir George Carteret[87] and John, Lord Berkeley.

Berkeley, who in addition to his interest in the gifted lands in New Jersey, held another interest in Shaftesbury's massive Carolina Proprietary. Perhaps Berkeley considered these vast holdings to be too much. In any case, he sold his half of New Jersey to the Quakers on 18 March 1673. In the same year, Charles issued a grant to the second Thomas, Lord Culpeper and Henry Bennett, Earl of Arlington, covering all lands in Virginia south of the Rappahannock River. On 4 March 1681, Charles II settled a substantial loan from William Penn's father with another proprietary grant consisting of a large tract that included the territory John Lord Berkeley had previously transferred to the Quakers. James II would complete his brother's policy of consolidating the kingdom's American possessions within revenue-generating proprietaries by forming the short-lived Dominion of New England in 1686.

In earlier ages, feudal lords protected themselves and their dominions by forming alliances with vassal partners. Cash-strapped Charles, in the course of implementing his brother's master plan, effectively modernized this ancient system by replacing its military component with an economic component. Abandoning the model that Thomas Jefferson later characterized as "a military system of defense," they formed alliances that served the financial interests of both the superior and inferior partners. This device represented a practical solution to an otherwise unsolvable problem. By organizing their New World dominions into proprietaries, the Stuarts opened the way for their wilderness lands to become revenue-generating assets, an objective that they were unable to accomplish themselves due to lack of money.

In the process of revamping feudalism to fit their needs, the Stuart kings established a version of the system that Edwin Sandys had

James Stewart, Duke of York as Lord High Admiral
(1633–1701)

promoted on behalf of the Virginia Company's investors. Both were geared to generate profits for the colony's owners. Both were carried forward by profit-seeking entrepreneurs. The common communal interest that qualified both entrepreneurial associations as Lockean bodies politic centered on their parallel interests in developing revenue-generating markets. Both assembled in legislative bodies where they defined their common good and enacted laws to accomplish it. In neither instance did the vast majority of the inhabitants of the territories in question have any say in the matter.

Charles II Signs the Charter of Pennsylvania, 1682

The Conflicting Plans of William Berkeley and Charles II

While Charles II's ministers were developing a colonial policy to generate revenue for the new king in London, William Berkeley was revamping the government in Virginia to maximize revenues for himself. According to Thomas Wertenbaker, "Upon receiving the news of the execution of Charles I, Sir William proclaimed Charles II King. And when, in 1652, a Parliamentary fleet sailed up the James to reduce the colony, he summoned the militia and prepared for a stubborn resistance. It was only when his Council

Anthony Ashley Cooper, 1ˢᵗ Lord Shaftesbury (1621–1683)

pointed out the folly of defying the might of Britain that he reluctantly agreed to surrender. But his soul was filled with bitterness. So, with the restoration of Charles II to the throne, when once more he was governor of Virginia, he was determined to permit no more representative government than his commission and instructions made necessary." He did this, Wertenbaker asserted, by corrupting Virginia's legislature:

> He took on himself "the sole nominating" of all civil and military officers picking out such persons as he thought would further his designs. Collectors', sheriffs' [and] justices' places were handed out to the Burgesses with a lavish hand. ... In this way he "gained upon and obliged" the "men of parts and estates" in the

Burgesses, and made them subservient to his will.... Sir William further bound his favorites to him by granting them great tracts of the best land.... The poor planters complained bitterly of the great sums voted by the Assembly for their own salaries, those of certain officers, and various other expenses.... The people were convinced that the heavy taxes served no other purpose than to enrich Berkeley's favorites.... Part of [Berkeley's] fortune came to him through a monopoly of the beaver trade with the Indians. He seems to have cashed in on this by licensing the traders on the frontier and taking a large part of their profits.[88]

Berkeley's success in solidifying his own establishment created a nettlesome obstruction for Charles II's Tory ministers who were laboring to implement James' larger scheme in London. In the meantime, these manipulations were beginning to draw the attention of a third party comprised of the mostly destitute residents of Virginia's untamed frontier. Richard Morton described the situation this way:

This grant (of the Northern Neck) brought resentment and great uneasiness in Virginia, even though the Northern Neck was to continue under the political control of the Virginia government. In spite of this opposition, the King in 1669 issued a new grant to the same region, which gave the proprietors large control over local government but left the final authority still in the hands of the government in Jamestown. *The Virginians, seeing in this another step toward creating a full proprietary government within the bounds of the Colony, were greatly disturbed.* When the King, at the request of the patentees, sent Berkeley orders early in 1670 to aid them in settling the region, Berkeley answered, in a letter to Secretary Arlington, that the power set forth in the new grant threatened the safety of the Virginia government, and that he had never "observed anything so much move the peoples' grief or passion, or which doth more put a stop to their industry than

John Colepeper, 1ˢᵗ Baron of Thoresway (__–1660)

their uncertainty whether they should make a country for the King or other proprietors."[89] (emphasis added)

This was the tense state of affairs when Thomas, Lord Culpeper, 2ⁿᵈ Baron of Thoresway joined the Council for Foreign Plantations on 20 March 1671. When the council was consolidated into "the Council of all affairs relating to Trade and Foreign Colonies and Plantations" under the direction of the Earl of Shaftesbury on 16 September 1672, Lord Thomas became its Vice President. Service on these panels acquainted Culpeper with the profitable nature of England's tobacco trade in Virginia. In this way, the financially pressed Tory came to perceive the colony as a source of revenue to settle a 12,000 pounds grant that was outstanding from Charles II to his deceased father, the 1ˢᵗ Baron of Thoresway.

In 1669, the men who sat in Virginia's beleaguered assembly dispatched Colonel Francis Moryson to England. His mission was to persuade the king to revoke the Northern Neck grant. Although he was not entirely successful in this effort, he did persuade the king to revise the grant so that it recognized all patents issued in the area prior to Charles II's restoration.[90] Lord Thomas had not deemed it worth his while to have his name included in the revised charter of 1669. But in the course of serving on the king's councils, he formed a different view of matter. By 1673, he was ready to act.

He began by securing formal recognition for his inherited interest in the revised 1669 charter—a grant that then had twenty-one years left in its term. He then enlisted the aid of Henry Bennett, the powerful Lord Arlington who had since 1662 served Charles II as Secretary of State, to solicit a second grant, this one seeking to control Virginia's lands below the Rappahannock River for thirty-one years from 10 March 1672.[91] Charles II acquiesced to Lord Thomas and Lord Henry's petition. Morton interpreted the award in these words:

If the Virginians thought that the King still had some consideration for them and that they had succeeded in putting an end to the threat of political and economic control by proprietors, they were soon rudely disillusioned. The final blow came in February 1672 when Charles II began making arrangements for granting the whole of Virginia, except the Northern Neck, to two of his favorites Henry Bennett, Earl of Arlington, and Thomas Lord Culpeper. The grant, dated February 25, 1673, and made for a period of thirty-one years, gave Arlington and Culpeper all lands in Virginia south of the Rappahannock River with all rents and arrears in rents of all lands since 1669. It gave them power to grant lands in fee simple and to confirm former grants; authority to establish counties, parishes, and towns; the status of "sole and absolute patrons" of all churches, with authority to establish churches, colleges, schools, and other institutions, and to nominate and present ministers and teachers, and to appoint all sheriffs, surveyors, and other officers of the Colony and of the counties.[92]

In September of 1674, Berkeley's assembly drafted a petition to the king pleading that he revoke this patent and asking him to re-confirm the rights and privileges of the colony. It then appointed two of its members, Thomas Ludwell and Robert Smith, to deliver the petition to His Majesty who seemed sympathetic. Drawing on desires made known by the colony's agents, the king's attorney and his solicitor general created a report preserving some of the colony's self-government rights.

Morton explained the document's contents: "The first two articles dealt with the problem uppermost in the people's mind. *They provided that the government of Virginia be enabled to buy the Northern Neck grant, and that 'the people of Virginia may be assured that they shall have no other dependence on the Crown*, nor be cantonized into parcels by grants made to particular persons'; that all land titles be confirmed, and that the fifty-acre headright for each immigrant be continued; that the Governor and Council be residents of Virginia, and should a deputy be chosen that he be selected from among the Councilors; that 'no manner of imposition or taxes shall be laid or imposed upon the inhabitants and proprietors there, but by the common consent of the Governor. Council, and Burgesses, as hath been hithertofore used.'"[93] (emphasis added)

As this work proceeded, Culpeper held discussions with Col. Moryson on the possible sale of the Northern Neck charter to Virginia as a corporation. At the same time, he negotiated a concession with the Virginian whereby he and Arlington agreed to relinquish all claims beyond the quitrents and escheats that Norwood had collected. This did not, however, signify that Culpeper was losing interest in Virginia. Indeed, at this hectic moment, he submitted a patent seeking William Berkeley's post as governor. Suspicious of Berkeley and eager to move forward with their reorganization, the

Thomas, 2nd Lord Culpeper (1635–1685)

council was happy to appoint one of their own to succeed him. But Berkeley had a powerful friend on the Privy Council—his brother. Therefore, on 8 July 1675 the lords of trade conferred upon Culpeper a lifetime appointment as Governor of Virginia to become effective upon Berkeley's death.

As the great reorganization proceeded in London, the political sands shifted in Virginia. This occurred when a man with special political skills began to organize the disgruntled members of its minor gentry and the destitute rabble, which inhabited the state of nature on Virginia's Indian-infested frontier. The *de facto* leader of this *posse comitatus* was the governor's kinsman Nathaniel Bacon.

Bacon's Rebellion

Nathaniel Bacon was a cousin to Governor William Berkeley's wife. Berkeley had welcomed the charismatic young aristocrat to Virginia in 1673, granting him a large tract of land on the unsettled western edge of the Tidewater colony. Two years later, Berkeley made a place for his wife's kinsman in his inner circle as a member of Virginia's council of state. Bacon apparently had something more in mind. When marauding Indians inflamed Virginia's wilderness boarders in the fall of 1675, he organized his neighbors into a private militia and set out to enforce the peace.

Bacon conducted his campaign in direct defiance of Governor Berkeley's orders. This placed Berkeley in a difficult position. If he moved against his disobedient councilor, he risked igniting a civil war with Bacon's increasingly hostile faction. If he allowed his young rival to defy him, he risked undermining the authority of his government. Berkeley tried to escape from this dilemma by handing the matter over to his friends in the assembly. He knew these men would take care of him because positions and prosperity depended on his good will. The assembly made a good effort at diffusing the crisis by declaring war on "bad" Indians. This tactic failed, however, when Bacon demanded a commission to lead the militia into the field against the bad Indians. When Berkeley refused to comply with his demand, Bacon again defied him. This time, he volunteered to lead *the people* against their Indian tormentors and to pay the cost of the campaign himself. When his frontier neighbors accepted his offer, Bacon resumed his post at the head of his rabble army.

Berkeley responded by assembling a company of three hundred "well-armed gentlemen" and marching out to Bacon's Henrico "headquarters." Bacon learned of Berkeley's approach in time to escape into the forest. Berkeley, who treated the event as a military victory, then declared Bacon a *rebel* and removing him from the council. Even as he isolated his footloose foe, Berkeley offered an olive branch to Bacon's followers by promising to pardon all of those who returned to their homes. His next concern was to reestablish the authority of his government, which he did by calling for new elections. This backfired, however, when Bacon's constituents elected him to represent them in the new assembly.

When the brazen legislator appeared to take his seat, Berkeley seized him and in court before the council, forced Bacon to apologize to him. Satisfied by this show of contrition, Berkeley pardoned the rebel and allowed him to return to the assembly. Bacon soon became embroiled in a debate over Indian policy. Unsatisfied with its outcome, Bacon stormed out of the hall. A short time later he returned with a regiment of armed followers. At Bacon's command, they surrounded the statehouse. Bacon then renewed his demands for his military commission. Again Berkeley refused. "Here," the governor shouted, bearing his breast, "shoot me before God, fair mark shoot." When Bacon did not shoot, Berkeley rewarded him with the commission. This time Bacon refused it, demanding instead that he be made General of all the colony's armies. When Berkeley refused this demand, the enraged Bacon threatened to shoot the captive burgesses. Berkeley ended a tense standoff by capitulating to Bacon's demand. Commission in hand, Bacon marched off to war against the Indians. Berkeley retired to his estate in disgust and frustration.

Now the commander of an army, Bacon asserted his authority as though he were the head of a new government. Concluding that *the people* were supreme, on 30 July 1676, he issued a "Declaration of the People" in which he accused Berkeley of corruption and misgovernment and demanded that he and his cronies surrender themselves to his tribunal. This proved to be a declaration of a war, which continued for four blistering months. During this "rebellion," Bacon's army chased Berkeley across the colony, burned his abandoned capital to the ground, and ransacked his estate and those of his wealthy allies. On 26 October, the energy of the rebel-

Nathaniel Bacon and His Followers Burning Jamestown, 1676

lion spent, Bacon suddenly died. Without his leadership, his rebellion collapsed and his followers drifted back to their homes and hovels.

Robert Beverly described Bacon's insurgency in these words:

The occasion of this rebellion is not easy to be discovered: But it is certain there were many things that concurred towards it. For it cannot be imagined, that upon the instigation of two or three traders only, who aimed at a monopoly of the Indian trade, as some pretend to say, the whole country would have fallen into so much distraction; in which people did not only hazard their necks by rebellion: But endeavored to ruin a Governor, whom they all entirely loved, and had unanimously chosen; a Gentleman who had devoted his whole life and estate to the service of the country; and against whom in thirty five years experience, there had never been one single complaint. Neither can it be supposed, that upon so slight grounds, they would make a choice of a leader they hardly knew, to oppose a gentleman, that had been so long, and so deservedly the darling of the people. *So that in all probability there was something else in the wind without which the body of the country had never been engaged in that insurrection.*

Four things may be reckoned to have been the main ingredients towards this intestine commotion, *viz.* First, the extreme low price of tobacco, and the ill usage of the planters in the exchange of goods for it, which the country, will all their earnest endeavors, could not remedy. Secondly, the splitting of the colony into proprieties, contrary to the original charters, and the extravagant taxes they were forced to undergo, to relieve themselves from those grants. Thirdly, the heavy restraints and burdens laid upon their trade by act of Parliament in England. Fourthly, the disturbance given by the Indians.[94]

Beverly's interpretation of Bacon's Rebellion reflected his perspective as a member of Berkeley's establishment. Thus, while he noticed the intrusions of the king's party and the disturbances of the *naturals* that sparked the uprising, he failed see any connection between the success of his own small circle in promoting its particular interests and Bacon's success in organizing a new body politic to pursue its own common good. In fact, Bacon's new political association was as much opposed to Berkeley's establishment as it was to Charles II's London Tories (not to mention the Indians on the frontier). Beverly may have been right, however, in his suggestion that the Lords of London triggered Bacon's movement by their efforts to change the colony's "ancient" ways. According to Beverly,

King Charles the Second, to gratify some nobles about him, made two great grants out of that country. These grants were not of the uncultivated woodland only, but also of plantations, which for many years had been seated and improved, under the encouragement of several charters granted by his royal ancestors to that colony. Those grants were distinguished by the names of the Northern and Southern Grants of Virginia, and the same men were concerns in both. They were kept dormant some years after they were made, and in the year 1674 begun to be put in execution. As soon as ever the country came to know this, they remonstrated against them; and the assembly drew up a humble address to his Majesty, complaining of the said grants, as derogatory to that colony, by his Majesty and his royal progenitors. They sent to England Mr. Secretary Ludwell and Colonel Park, as their agents to address the King to vacate those grants. And the better to defray that charge, they laid a tax of fifty pounds of tobacco per poll, for two years together, over and above all other taxes, which was an excessive burden...which taxes and amercements fell heaviest on the poor peoples, the effect of whose labor would not cloth their wives and children. This made them desperately uneasy, especially when, after a whole year's patience under all these pressures, they had no encouragement from their agents in England.[95]

The collapse of Bacon's movement did not settle matters between Charles II's Tories and William Berkeley.

The charter revision of 1675 had provided a framework in which this conflict might have been resolved. Unfortunately, Bacon's rebellion erupted before the new charter was released. When it was over, the king was in a different frame of mind. Suppressing the conciliatory document his attorney and his solicitor general had drawn, Charles II instead issued a statement acknowledging the existing land titles and the dependence of the colony "upon the crown of England, under the rule and government of such governors as we…shall from time to time appoint."[96] Two years passed before this document finally appeared. In the interim, the unhappy king, disturbed by the state of affairs in Virginia and anxious to complete the implementation of his grand strategy, summoned Governor Berkeley to England. The chastened governor finally departed Virginia on 5 May 1677. He died two months later.

The Northern Neck Proprietary

The king and his men publicly lamented Berkeley's death. In private, they celebrated the opportunity it afforded to push their program forward. Lord Culpeper was given his oath of office in a ceremony before the Privy Council on 20 July 1677. The order was then issued that he leave at once for Virginia where the door was now open for the king to reassert his authority. This was not, however, Lord Thomas' immediate concern. Although he was now the king's man in Virginia, his view of the colony was colored by his proprietary interests. That is, Lord Culpeper was now in position to build his personal fortune. To properly exploit the opportunity, he no doubt wanted the new charter to reflect his proprietary interests. It seems likely, therefore, that he involved himself in the charter's revision.

The charter was released in the middle of 1678. By then England was occupied with the Popish Plot alleged against Titus Oates. This further delayed Lord Thomas. Finally, under threat of termination, he boarded his ship and on 13 February 1680 departed for Virginia. He arrived in Virginia on 3 May. He remained there long enough to confirm the potential of his proprietary. Having satisfied himself on this critical point, he returned to England, departing Virginia on 11 August. Back in England, he occupied himself buying up the interests of his fellow proprietors. He completed this business during the summer of 1681. On 21 July he was issued a deed as sole proprietor of the Northern Neck. His deed to the Arlington Grant is dated 10 September.

Culpeper returned to his post for a final brief tour in December 1682. His first acts upon arriving were to assert his proprietary right as "sole owner" of the Northern Neck and to appoint a "Receiver General" to collect duties owed him above the Rappahannock River and below the Potomac River. Then, in May of 1683, Culpeper left Virginia for good. With his unauthorized departure, he forfeited his office and his salary as governor. He compensated himself for this loss by converting the Arlington charter into a twenty-one-year pension at 600 pounds per year. While he completed this transaction, his agent in Virginia persuaded the assembly to reopen negotiations for the purchase of the Northern Neck charter. These negotiations stumbled, however, when a common price could not be established. They failed when it was determined that the colony could not make the purchase in a corporate capacity.

Culpeper concluded the final transaction in his Virginia business six months before his death at the age of fifty-four. On 10 July 1688, James II renewed his Northern Neck patent, which then had less than two years remaining in its term. This asset was to pass through a series of litigations initiated first by Lady Culpeper and then by Lord Thomas' disinherited brother John. The legal cloud that enshrouded the property finally dissipated on 11 January 1693 when the king's attorney general, Sir John Somers, concluded that "the said grant did pass in all the usual methods of grants of that nature and that the petitioners Margaret Lady Culpeper, Thomas

Lord Fairfax, Katherine his wife and Alexander Culpeper, Esqr. be permitted to enjoy the benefits of the said letters patents according to law, so as they keep strictly to the tenor thereof, in execution of the several powers and authorities thereby granted; of which all persons whom it may concern are to take notice."[97]

SEVEN

Colonel Richard Lee's Submission to Lord Fairfax

———•·•———

Each pursuing the other's prize, it was inevitable that Sir William would come into conflict with the Crown. And since the prize in question involved the well-being of the rabble that existed beneath the colony's self-centered establishment, it was equally inevitable that the maneuverings of the governor and James Stewart would offend them. Their subsequent rebellion under the leadership of Nathaniel Bacon sealed Berkeley's fate. In the process, it opened the door to another of the colony's notorious characters—Thomas, 2nd Lord Culpeper. Opportunity opened to Lord Thomas as Charles' calculating brother implemented his plan to distribute England's new world territories under grants to Charles' wealthiest allies. While James' plan was ripening for Culpeper, class conflict between the Old Dominion's governing class and the neglected inhabitants of its dangerous frontier set the stage for Colonel Lee. Thirty years later the introspective gentleman from Virginia's Northern Neck resolved the still-simmering conflict for himself and his peers in Virginia's governing class by transferring his allegiance to the Lords Fairfax and thereby aligning himself with the ancient and hereditary social system of Mother England. This transfer of allegiance completed the birth of Virginia's *aristocracy*.

———•·•———

I T TOOK THOMAS, 5ᵀᴴ LORD FAIRFAX, Culpeper's son-in-law, seven years more to establish his authority under his grant. "By 1700," Burton Hendrick reported, "not a solitary planter had attorned to the new proprietor—that is, had shifted his feudal allegiance to the Fairfax family."[98] This observation shows that the feudal right that was sustained in England by *common custom* was a matter of *voluntary cooperation* in Virginia. Failing to see advantage in a subservient relationship to an absentee lord, Virginia's headmen simply refused to acknowledge it. Beverly gave this account of the unexpected change in the Fairfaxes' fortunes:

"Upon the death of Mr. Secretary Spencer, he [Fairfax] engaged another noted gentleman, an old stander in that country, Col. Philip Ludwell who was then in England. He went over with this grant in the year 1690, and set up an office in the Neck, claiming some escheats; but he likewise could make nothing of it…after him Col. George Brent and Col. William Fitz-Hugh, that were likewise inhabitants of the said Neck, were employed in that affair: but succeeded no better than their predecessors. The people in the meanwhile, complained frequently to their assemblies, who at last made another address to the King; but there being no agent in England to prosecute it, that likewise miscarried. At last, Colonel Richard Lee, one of the council, an inhabitant of the Northern Neck, privately made a composition with the proprietors themselves for his own land. This broke the Ice, and several were induced to follow so great an example; so that by degrees, they were generally brought to pay their quitrents into the hands of the proprietors' agents. And now at last it is managed for them by Col. Robert Carter, another of the Council, and one of the greatest freeholders of that propriety."[99]

"What Richard's attorning meant," Hendrick explained, "was that he acknowledged the Fairfax family as liege lord, and was prepared to pay those annual quitrents formerly paid to the king. The

Thomas, 5th Lord Fairfax
(1657–1709)

practical outcome was to destroy the head-right system in this part of Virginia. Henceforth settlers were to obtain land in the Northern Neck from the Fairfax family, on lease, not freehold."[100] This change in the mode of land ownership was, according to Hendrick, the foundation on which "the celebrated Virginia aristocracy" developed. Hendrick was correct in his conclusion, but his account of the birthing act was incomplete. In fact, the Virginia's aristocracy rested on something far more sublime than mere law. This becomes clear upon closer inspection of Richard Lee's act of submission.

The homage Lee chose to pay Thomas, Lord Fairfax did more than change the mode in which he held his land. In acknowledging the Fairfax family as his liege lord, Lee also affirmed his subjection under the King of England. This evidently suited Lee. Why? "Everything known of the second Richard," Hendrick reported, "portrays a man thoughtful, serious, quiet, devoted to the domestic

Richard Lee II (1647–1714)

virtues, deeply loyal in his political convictions, prepared at times, to sacrifice personal fortune for things in which he believed."[101] In the course of long and careful reflection, this thoughtful man seems to have discovered that he had a higher regard for their lordships in England than for the rabble in Virginia. He may have realized that by endorsing the hierarchical order that the king sustained, he would establish himself within it.

There was quite possibly a political component in Lee's calculation. Culpeper had failed to resolve the conflict between the London lords and Virginia's oligarchy. By the time of Richard's attorning, it had been simmering for thirty years. Perceiving himself as part of the governing class that William Berkeley had created,

Lee may have decided to make symbolic peace with his lordships. This was hardly painful since the superiors of the system to whom he was submitting were far enough removed that they could have little impact on his personal sovereignty.

Lee's gesture attracted the attention of his peers. Ruminating on it, they came around to his way of thinking. One influenced another until the idea was common among the colony's best men. Then they were Virginia's *aristocracy*. Not only did they act the part, they conducted the business of their community in these terms. "As the colony increased," Thomas Jefferson reported in his *Notes on Virginia*, "and individual applications for land multiplied, it was found to give too much occupation to the general assembly to enquire into and execute the grant in every special case. They therefore thought it better to establish general rules, according to which all grants should be made, and to leave to the governor the execution of them, under these rules. *This they did by what have been usually called the land laws, amending them from time to time, as their defects were developed.*"[102] (emphasis added)

In the course of this dispersed process, Virginia's aristocrats developed a system of land laws that suited their needs. In the Northern Neck, grants were made by their Fairfax Lords. These lands were held of them. Tenants on these lands paid them their quitrent duties. If they died without heirs, their lands escheated (transferred back) to the Fairfaxes. The Fairfaxes in turn held of the king and had their own duties to their liege lord. A different system, however, governed below the Rappahannock. There, the governor reviewed and approved patents submitted by individual citizens and later by corporations. These were the *king's* lands. The governor's agents collected quitrents on these parcels in the name of the king. "As to the tenure," Edmund Pendleton wrote in his 26 August 1776 letter to Jefferson, "It was the slavish nature of the feuds which made them oppressive to the tenant and inconsistent with freedom, and the establishment of a military force independent of the legislature, which proved injurious to the community, but I confess I am not able to discover disgrace to the tenant or injury to the society from their holding of the commonwealth, upon terms of paying a small certain annual sum disposable for the common benefit, by their own representatives: nor what this will retain of the old feuds?"[103]

Jefferson conceded that the feud existed in colonial Virginia. "How far our acts of assembly or acceptance of grants may have converted lands which were allodial into feuds I have never considered," Jefferson confessed in his 13 August 1776 letter to Pendleton. Jefferson suggested in this comment that although it was part of the legal institute, its form was shaped as much by custom as by statute. These customs obviously differed from place to place. The northern perimeter of the colony conformed to conditions defined by the proprietary grant held by the Fairfax family until the American Revolution. Those who lived on these lands paid quitrents to Lord Fairfax's agents. Those who lived on the great bulk of the land outside the Northern Neck Proprietary were effectively tenants of the King of England. They would have paid their quitrents to his agents within the colonial government. If Jefferson was correct in his observations to Pendleton, some colonial lands were owned without superior. Owners of these tracts would have paid taxes to colonial government. When they died, law and custom dictated they pass their landed property to their eldest son or to their nearest male heir. This confusing system solidified through one hundred years of colonial rule.

EIGHT

The Squirearchy in the Revolutionary Era

By the time Thomas Jefferson wrote his draft for the *Declaration of Independence*, Virginia had been the *Old Dominion* for near fourscore years. The colony was still growing and dividing as it had during its first century. More than a century and a half after its first palisades were erected, its western frontier still stretched into the unknown. But during this time the Tidewater had been tamed, its forests cleared and its land brought under cultivation. The place where a majority of its earliest adventurers had perished from lack of food, disease, and warfare with hostile Indians had been transformed into a haven. The land that comprised it was still held in many instances by the descendents of its original owners. These individuals constituted a small, closed circle that was set apart from the rest of the community not just by wealth and position. Time and experience had instilled in these men and their families a frame of mind that caused them to see the world in a way that other members of their households could not. The patriarchs of the Old Dominion—men like Archibald Cary, Peyton Randolph, and Edmund Pendleton—were raised from birth to preserve their *community*, which they saw in terms of the difficulties of its founding and the economic and social patterns that had allowed it to surmount these difficulties. As public administrators, they endeavored to maintain the ways of life that had over time produced peace and prosperity. These civic-minded men defended the colony's boarders, maintained its marketplaces, protected its citizens' property, and distributed justice according to its written laws and traditions. By doing these things, Virginia's aristocrats—model citizens in the Aristotelian sense—promoted the common good.

———————

E. C. DUNSTAN[104] referred to the Old Dominion in the generation preceding the American Revolution as a "squirearchy," a "self-perpetuating oligarchy of plantation owners." About this oligarchy, Robert P. Sutton observed: "More than in any other colony except perhaps South Carolina, the gentry monopolized Virginia's wealth by regulating its system of tobacco production and determining its land sales. They set standards of polite social behavior and were leaders of Virginia's intellectual and cultural life. In political matters they occupied all the Old Dominion's important offices from the county court to the governor's council. Most importantly, the colony's gentry was a homogenous group of adult white men of closely related families, a small, self-conscious social minority of probably not more than five percent of the population.... Yet," he added, "despite the power, they maintained an extraordinarily high sense of stewardship and responsibility."[105]

The following summary* of Virginia society in the late-colonial period is, with some editing, Dunstan's account:

By the middle of the eighteenth century the balance of power in the colony had shifted from the Royal Governor in Williamsburg to a closed circle formed by these men. To promote harmony, and to assure the smooth functioning of local government, the Royal

---

The passage excerpted from E.C. Dunstan's monograph is used with permission from the Alexandria Historical Society. The author would like to give special thanks to President Audrey Davis and Historian Michael Miller for their assistance in this matter.

Governor had become accustomed to defer to their wishes. By the same token, it suited their interests to cooperate with the Governor who was the King's personal representative. As the King's agent, the Governor could, for example, facilitate the patents they filed on new lands and the recording of their deeds. As head of the government, he was also the center of society and ceremony, which had particular significance during sessions of the General Assembly when they convened as Burgesses to practice their politics and oversee the colony's business.

In the course of the previous century, these men had become a governing class. They were raised with the understanding that when they came of age they would manage the government. Many were from families that had migrated to Virginia following Charles I's defeat in the English civil war. Several returned to England to be educated. Reading Magna Carta and English common law, they learned to appreciate their rights and responsibilities as Englishmen. They supplemented this fundamental knowledge by studying English history, ancient history, and theories of government. This training taught them that they would promote the common good by preserving the principles of government defined in the English constitution.

As gentlemen justices, they had two kinds of responsibilities. First, they served as justices of the peace with jurisdiction over petty infractions of the law. Their standing in society gave them a special advantage in mediating settlements between litigants within the community. They saw to it that cases were handled quickly, inexpensively, and with a minimum of damage to social cohesion. This method of doing justice was acceptable to a citizenry that was accustomed to the proceedings of *common law*.

Their more weighty responsibility was to serve on the county court. These courts had dual roles as instruments of local government. In some respects they functioned as a legislative body. They maintained the list of the county's taxable residents (tithables) and levied the taxes necessary to support the operation of the county government. They also had responsibility for planning, funding, building, and maintaining county structures. Included among these were buildings, bridges, roads, and ferries. Beyond these administrative functions, they served as a judicial body having jurisdiction for most cases "at common law or chancery." The court also served as a court of record for filing of deeds, mortgages, indentures, wills, and legal contracts.

The Governor appointed a member of the court to serve as sheriff. The sheriff was the chief law enforcement officer of the county and the chief administrative officer of the court. The Governor was careful to remain on good terms with the sheriff who, sharing the Governor's interest in preserving the peace, tended to reciprocate with his own gestures of good will. The term of service was one year, but appointments could be renewed and usually were. The court had authority to appoint the county tobacco inspectors. The court also appointed officers to the militia and frequently appointed its own members to serve in these positions.

County officers, whether civil, military, or ecclesiastical, were required to be members of the established Church. Because of their standing in the community, gentlemen justices were frequently vestrymen in their local parishes. Since there were no Archbishops in colonial Virginia, parish vestries had full responsibility for managing the affairs of the church. These extended from constructing church buildings, to contracting with the clergy, to providing for parish indigents.

Qualified freeholders in each county were entitled to elect two representatives to the lower house of the Virginia Assembly. A freeholder was a free, white male over the age of twenty-one (and a member of the Church of England) who had owned during the previous year either one hundred acres of unimproved land, twenty-five acres of improved land, or a lot in a town. Through these qualifications, the franchise to vote was restricted to established, taxpaying members of the community and the core of the state's militia. The concept of freeholder had been framed in 1619, five years before Virginia was made a Royal Colony. By 1774, it had therefore become an ancient and venerated part of Virginia's common law.

On Election Day, the candidates, the sheriff, and usually several gentlemen justices sat at a table where the voting was done. Each voter gave his name to the sheriff, who repeated it and asked his preference. When the voter announced his choice, the sheriff recorded it and the candidate receiving the vote rose and thanked the voter for his support. To be elected, a candidate had to court the votes of the small and medium freeholders. They did this by meeting with the yeomanry and trading views on important issues. Once elected, a candidate became a member of the House of Burgesses. The House of Burgesses' Committee of Privileges and Elections of the House examined the credentials of each member and investigated disputed elections. Partly because of the intermediation of this committee, it was difficult for the Governor to build a block of loyal supporter in the Assembly.

Members of the House of Burgesses elected a presiding officer known as the "Speaker" and twelve other eminent colleagues to serve on the Privy Council. The twelve-man Privy Council represented the upper house of the Assembly. Members of the Privy Council received their commission from the Governor and were presided over by the Governor. The Council also served as the General Court of the colony. It met twice a year in this capacity to hear cases considered too serious to be tried in county court and to hear appeals to cases tried in county court. The Attorney General, who was the chief law enforcement agent of the colony, was nominated by the House from among its members and received appointment by the Governor. The lower house also nominated one of its members to serve as Treasurer of the Colony. The Governor likewise approved this nomination and made the appointment. Among the responsibilities of the Treasurer of the Colony was to pay the Governor's salary.

Gentlemen at a Meet in Colonial Virginia, Circa 1760

County governments were financed by head taxes, but the colonial government—with the exception of the Fairfax Proprietary—was financed by land taxes (quitrents) payable annually to the Treasurer of the Colony. The rate was two shillings per hundred acres of land acquired by deed (patent) from the Governor. In this way, the colonial government maintained the feudal form inherited from the Mother Country.

The King could veto any act of the Assembly within three years of enactment.

It is evident from Dunstan's description that Virginia's closed agrarian society and its colonial government were both configured in ways that settled power in the hands of its leading citizens. This naturally increased the influence of the leading men in the Tidewater area because they were the best established, the largest landholders, and the colony's wealthiest individuals. In the years leading up to the American Revolution, even the colonial governor was subject to the will of this closed circle of peers. Powerful though they were, they were also responsible stewards. The commonality of the community's interests together with the regular, unchanging pattern of life simplified the task for the gentlemen justices who guided it. They presided like fathers over an extended, largely cohesive family. They were thus able to administer their dominions with minimal coercion or division.

These characteristics changed as the society opened and the interests of its members dispersed. In the course of this evolution, which young Thomas Jefferson quietly promoted as a private revolutionary and which George Mason publicly accommodated as an enlightened citizen, the gentlemen justices of the squirearchy were replaced by members of a *political* class. This process was hastened by western migration encouraged by the financial depression that engulfed the Tidewater after the revolution. As this change occurred, the common good gradually came to be defined in terms of the interests of competing regional and political factions. Eventually, the aristocracy that dominated affairs in the colonial era lost its significance and finally drifted out of sight.

NINE

Thomas Jefferson's Other Rebellion

Severing the bands that tied it to England made the agrarian system in the Old Dominion economically untenable. This was not its only problem. In the new *Jeffersonian* political logic, it was also effectively a fault to promote the well-being of the community over the rights of its individual members. The end was therefore at hand for Virginia's colonial *squirearchy*. Thomas Jefferson for one believed that it was necessary to dismantle its "pseudo-aristocracy" to make way for a new republican society. Few people are aware that Jefferson ended his participation in the rebellion that John Adams so skillfully precipitated five years before the American victory at Yorktown. Honoring a commitment to his anxious wife, Jefferson returned to Virginia two months after the Continental Congress revised and ratified his *Declaration of Independence*. He stopped at Monticello to collect his family before traveling on to Williamsburg. When the new General Assembly convened on 7 October 1776, Jefferson launched a carefully constructed campaign against Virginia's colonial hierarchy. Jefferson's *other* rebellion would dominate his attention and his efforts for the next three years. Although his plan failed, his objectives were accomplished over time. Twenty years later, a similar concern would inspire him to launch "the second American Revolution." In winning this insurgency,

Jefferson completed the transformation of his country into a modern *political society*.

———•———

THOMAS JEFFERSON undertook to replace the government Virginia's aristocrats operated and to uproot the society they maintained by making it impossible for them to pass their landed estates intact to their heirs. Why? He saw Virginia's hereditary hierarchy as a reproduction of the English social system, which he condemned for being conducive to tyranny.

How could he hold this view when he was part of the social hierarchy? Jefferson was connected to the inner circle through his mother, a cousin of Peyton Randolph, and through his wife, Martha Wayles, whose father, John Wayles, owned 17,000 acres on the James River and in the western part of the colony. But he was not what Sutton called a "Tuckahoe." Tuckahoes were mature men of substantial wealth, large planters, and slaveholders whose properties were located north of the James in the upper Tidewater area. In the quarter century prior to the War of Independence, political power in the Old Dominion had become concentrated in the hands of the "gentlemen justices" who resided in this region. These included Peyton Randolph, Archibald Cary, Richard Bland, Edmund Pendleton, George Washington, George Mason, and Jefferson's college friend John Page. The young man from the frontier was an outsider to this small society despite his blood connection to it.

The Seeds of Jefferson's Other Rebellion

Jefferson unknowingly sewed the seeds of his rebellion against his kinsmen and their social system during the summer of 1774. The stage had been set in a tumultuous sequence of events that began the previous December when a mob of Boston radicals dumped

The Burgesses Meeting at Raleigh Tavern

a cargo of British tea into Boston Harbor. Outraged, Parliament demanded that the perpetrators surrender themselves to justice and that restitution be made for the property they had destroyed. Should these demands go unmet, Parliament warned, the Port of Boston would be closed. The deadline for compliance was 1 June. The House of Burgesses imported this crisis into Virginia by designating June 1 as a day of fasting and prayer. Stern Lord Dunmore, acting governor of the colony, reacted by proroguing the assembly. The unseated burgesses, retiring to the Raleigh Tavern, voted to revive "The Association to Interdict trade with Britain." They went on to approve a recommendation from their committee of correspondence, of which Jefferson was a member, proposing another congress of the colonies and recommending that the counties of Virginia elect delegates to convene in Williamsburg on 1 August for the purpose of administering the business of the colony. Having settled on this plan of action, Jefferson retired to Monticello. In the library of his unfinished mansion he drafted a non-importation proposal for the freeholders of Albemarle County and "instructions" for Virginia's delegates to the said congress.

This second document proved not to be a set of instructions, but rather an enumeration of the Parliamentary acts that were, in Jefferson's view, *illegal*. In preparing to write the document, Jefferson probably reread the paper his cousin Richard Bland had written eight years earlier. In *An Inquiry into the Rights of the British Colonies*, Bland asserted that individuals, "though they submit to the laws so long as they remain members of the society, yet they retain so much of their natural freedom as to have a right to retire from the society, to renounce the benefits of it, to enter into another society, and to settle in another country; for their engagement to the society, and their submission to the public authority of the state, do not oblige them to continue in it longer than they find it will conduce to their happiness, which they have a natural right to promote. This Natural Right remains with every man, and he cannot justly be deprived of it by any civil authority."[106]

Jefferson interpreted this and said, "America was conquered, and her settlements made, and firmly established, at the expense of individuals, and not of the British public. Their own blood was spilt in acquiring lands for their settlement, their own fortunes expended in making that settlement effectual; and for themselves they fought, for themselves they conquered, and for themselves alone they have right to hold."[107] Having issued this challenge to Parliament, Jefferson trumped it in his conclusion: "But that we do not point out to his majesty the injustice of these acts, with intent to rest on that principle the cause of their nullity; but to show that experience confirms the propriety of those political principles which exempt us from the jurisdiction of the British Parliament. *The true ground on which we declare these acts void is, that the British Parliament has no right to exercise authority over us.*"[108] (emphasis added)

Jefferson thus followed Bland's reasoning to create what is called here an *argument from sovereignty*. In advancing this argument, Jefferson distinguished himself from his patriotic peers in the first Continental Congress, who would spend September and October of 1774 debating whether—in addition to violating their *constitutional rights*—Parliament was violating the *natural rights* of His Majesty's American subjects. John Adams launched this debate when he proposed that the colonials claim rights by *Nature* as well as by the British Constitution and the common law. Adams won this debate after Congress adjourned by incorporating both claims into what is known today as the *Declaration of Rights and Grievances*.[109]

Jefferson's Argument from Sovereignty

Why did Jefferson formulate Bland's analysis into an argument from sovereignty instead of Adams' *argument from right*? Jefferson, like everyone else, had his own sense of things. His view of the world and his interpretation of the events unfolding in it were shaped by the bent of his character. The bent of Jefferson's character caused him to resent the presumptuous claims of England's kings to land that men like his father risked their lives and fortunes to settle. It also caused him to reject Parliament's authority to make laws that infringed on his personal sovereignty. The frame of his mind, in other words, inclined him to support the radicals who were rebelling against British authority in Boston. Under these circumstances, it did not matter which class of rights Parliament was violating. The issue, for Jefferson at least, was that his peers in Virginia's governing hierarchy agree that Parliament had no authority to meddle in the internal affairs of the *sovereign* American People.

Jefferson remained in anxious seclusion as the delegates of the Virginia Convention considered and rejected his denial that England had a rightful authority to govern the American colonies. He continued in seclusion for another eight months after this understandably upsetting repudiation of his position. During this time, Jefferson must have considered the parallels between the hereditary system of England—a system that he had irreconcilably condemned—and the hierarchical order of his own society. Were not the problems with the goose the same with the gander?

It seems likely that Jefferson would have asked himself this question during the fall of 1774. Although it may have taken him a year to answer it, he had probably done so by the fall of 1775 when he set off to replace Peyton Randolph in the Philadelphia Congress. By then, he had concluded that the tyranny he perceived in England's monarchical system was also manifest in Virginia's squirearchy. When he reached Philadelphia, he found eminent members of the patriotic movement freely exchanging ideas about the proper form for a new government. This opened the door for Jefferson to take up the matter himself.

Jefferson's Other Rebellion

Jefferson's concern was subtly different from that of his congressional colleagues. Everyone wanted to eliminate the tyranny of the English monarchy, but Jefferson also wanted to prevent tyranny by Virginia's "pseudo-aristocracy." Like John Adams, Jefferson favored a republican form of government because it would allow *the people* to elect better men to define the common good and to make the laws to accomplish it. Jefferson feared, however, that the right sort of men would not ascend to leadership in the new government in Virginia if its colonial hierarchy retained its power and influence.

*Thomas Jefferson Writing the Declaration
of Independence, 1776*

Jefferson contemplated this problem through the winter of 1776. On the way back to Philadelphia in May of that year he produced the first of several drafts of his plan for a new government in Virginia. As he refined this plan through successive drafts, his thoughts crystallized on how to prevent Virginia's oligarchs from dominating and stifling its new social and political systems. Jefferson aimed to accomplish this by incorporating three key provisions into the state's new constitution.

The First Phase

Jefferson's first objective was to eliminate the tenure system on which the colony's land laws rested. He meant to accomplish this by giving settlers of the state's vast western territories full ownership of the land they claimed. Jefferson supplemented this provision with a system of proportional representation that would shift political power away from the Tidewater as the population of the state's western lands increased. To these provisions Jefferson attached a comprehensive plan to reform Virginia's judiciary.

Jefferson followed Locke in recognizing a fundamental relationship between property and government. But where Locke asserted that individuals join together in society to preserve their (natural right to own and enjoy) property, Jefferson saw that the accumulation of (real) property produced political power. And where Locke made the purpose of government to protect individual rights to property, Jefferson designed political procedures to distribute real property in a way that would keep political power from pooling in the hands of individuals whom he distrusted as group.

He saw his plan for proportional representation as a mechanism for constituting an electorate of yeoman farmers that would share his independent spirit and enlightened self-interests. These *republicans* would grow in numbers, become the majority, and eventually take control of the government. In this process they would accumulate the power previously exercised by colonial Virginia's Tidewater aristocracy and eliminate it as a threat to the state's emerging republican society.

The third key provision in Jefferson's plan for the new government of Virginia reconstituted the state's anti-republican judiciary. The county courts, which played a central role in the management of local affairs, represented an area of special concern. County magistrates held essentially hereditary positions and wielded pervasive powers. Among the most dangerous in Jefferson's view was their power to modify sentences as prescribed in the written law. In Jefferson's eyes this was an abuse of power by individuals who were not answerable *to the people.* To prevent amateur jurists from undercutting the written law with unschooled opinions, Jefferson provided for a High Court of Chancery to be run by trained lawyers selected by the state's executive and his Privy counsel. Following the practice of common law Jefferson included a provision for the removal of judges for "misbehavior." These practical first steps would limit the authority of the county justices and, over time, eliminate their hereditary seats.

Jefferson gave the final draft of his *Constitution for the State Virginia* to his trusted friend and political ally, George Wythe, who carried it with him to Williamsburg. Wythe delivered Jefferson's plan to the Virginia Convention on 23 June 1776. The squires who dominated this body unwittingly thwarted his rebellion against them by enacting George Mason's alternative plans few days later.

The Second Phase

By the time the Williamsburg convention passed over Jefferson's constitution, Jefferson's attention had shifted to a more urgent matter. He had learned on 29 June that the beyond-the-veil efforts he had spent to avoid reelection to the Continental Congress had failed and that the convention had elected him to serve second term. This was awful news since he had promised his anxious wife that he would retire from national politics and return home to his family when his term ended in August. Fearing the impact his reelection would have on his "domestic affairs," he rushed a panicked letter to Edmund Pendleton. In this letter he pleaded that circumstances in his household required that he be excused.

This uncharacteristically blunt appeal marked the beginning of a second phase in Jefferson's *other* rebellion. Jefferson revised his plan to dismantle Virginia's ruling oligarchy in the course of a probing correspondence with Pendleton that occupied the two men during July and August of 1776. It seems ironic given Jefferson's intentions that Pendleton wanted Jefferson to join Virginia's new government where he could *"exercise [his] talents for the nurture of Our new Constitution, which will require all the Attention of its friends to prune exuberances and Cherish the Plant."* At first, Jefferson resisted, but when he learned that he had been excused from serving again in Philadelphia, his attitude changed. In the course of his exchange with Pendleton, Jefferson realized that he could accomplish his objective by pushing a carefully designed program of legislation through the new assembly. "We have it in our power," he explained to Pendleton in confirming that he would join the new legislature, "to make it what it ought to be for the public good."

Pendleton was, of course, not a republican and did not support the legislative program Jefferson assembled between the end of August and the beginning of October. As the dean of Virginia's ruling oligarchy, he thought in terms of fine-tuning a system that had sustained the Old Dominion through its long, settling history. It never seems to have occurred to him that a member of his own class would use his place in the legislature to undermine a political system that did in fact work.

The Third Phase

The third phase of Jefferson's rebellion against Virginia's aristocracy began when he took his seat in the new legislature. As soon as he was seated, Jefferson commenced his legislative campaign. During the first eight weeks of the session, Jefferson submitted fifteen bills, which he drafted personally, aided in drafting, or revised. Taken together, these measures would, if enacted, accomplish what Jefferson had tried to do in his prior plan of government. In this sense, Jefferson's legislative initiative was a continuation of his earlier effort to obstruct tyranny. As he guided measure after measure through the legislative process, it appears that Jefferson began to see that he was doing more than merely obstructing tyrants. During this eight-week whirlwind campaign, Jefferson came to see that he was superintending a new construction.

This transformation in Jefferson's thinking probably occurred during his battle with Carter Braxton over the division of Fincastle County. Jefferson won this legislative battle when he succeeded in incorporating into the measure's final draft an amendment giving inhabitants of the new counties the right to vote if they possessed the usual property qualifications "altho' no legal title in the land shall have been conveyed to such possessor." Giving settlers of these lands title to the land they claimed allowed them to become voting members of Virginia's new political society. Perhaps it was at the moment of victory that Jefferson recognized that these intrepid pioneers—fearless, freedom-loving men like his father—were his constituents. Able now to relate to *the people*, he became a champion of government by *their* consent. At this late moment, Jefferson became a *republican*.

The Fourth Phase

Noteworthy among the avalanche of legislation that Jefferson introduced was his bill for revising the law. Upon its enactment, Jefferson was named to the committee of the revisers. The fourth and final phase of Jefferson's rebellion against Virginia's ancient system began when he convened this committee in Fredericksburg in January of 1777. Jefferson continued quietly in this work for more than two years. Laboring alone in his library at Monticello, he modernized the code's outdated language and streamlined its common law statutes. As he redrafted bill after bill, he must have grappled with a larger, more abstract problem. How could he preserve this new society of yeoman farmers? How could he, in other words, maintain his "well-ordered" republic? The solution he found is arguably his most creative political idea. In proposing to institute a system of public education, he unknowingly endorsed an idea central to Plato's republic. Both men sought to protect their political creations by creating a governing class. Plato called these men "philosopher kings." Jefferson called them an "aristoi of merit and talent." Where Plato intended to create a standing army of "guardians" to watch over his docile and contented flock, recipients of Jefferson's public education would learn to be *good* citizens. For Jefferson "good" meant recognizing tyranny and obstructing those who tried to create it.

Jefferson did not know in 1778 when he stumbled upon Plato's long-lost nostrum that a political organization was needed for its implementation. He would have this revelation during his enlightening experience in France where politics became for him a science and where Jefferson became at last the *political* agent. When he returned from France, Jefferson joined President George Washington's cabinet as the first Secretary of State. A member of the president's inner circle of advisors, Jefferson soon discovered that America's new "aristoi of merit and talent" contained the same kind of tyrants that had filled Virginia's colonial aristocracy. Alarmed and outraged he resigned from the cabinet and launched—and won—a "Second American Revolution." The rest is history.

Endnotes

1. Jordan, *White Cargo*, 235.
2. Ibid., 236.
3. The First Charter of Virginia, issued 10 April 1606, names the licensees in its first paragraph. It reads: "JAMES, by the Grace of God, King of England, Scotland, France and Ireland, Defender of the Faith, &c. WHEREAS our loving and well-disposed Subjects, *Sir Thomas Gates*, and *Sir George Somers*, Knights, *Richard Hackluit*, Clerk, Prebendary of Westminster, and *Edward-Maria Wingfield*, *Thomas Hanham* and *Ralegh Gilbert*, Esqrs. *William Parker*, and *George Popham*, Gentlemen, and divers others of our loving Subjects, have been humble Suitors unto us, that We would vouchsafe unto them our Licence, to make Habitation, Plantation, and to deduce a colony of sundry of our People into that part of America commonly called VIRGINIA, and other parts and Territories in America, either appertaining unto us, or which are not now actually possessed by any Christian Prince or People, situate, lying, and being all along the Sea Coasts, between four and thirty Degrees of Northerly Latitude from the Equinoctial Line, and five and forty Degrees of the same Latitude, and in the main Land between the same four and thirty and five and forty Degrees, and the Islands "hereunto adjacent, or within one hundred Miles of the Coast thereof...." Thorpe, *Federal and State Constitutions*.
4. Dabney, *Virginius*, 10. It is more accurate to say that these assets remained the property of the company, which distributed food from its store as needed by its tenants. Perhaps half of these were indentured servants who had traded four to five years of their labor for passage to the New World.
5. Rubin, *Virginia*, 5.
6. Hamor, *A True Discourse*, 17.

7. Ibid., 16.
8. From the Ferrar Papers, 40-1501, Magdelene College Library, reproduced in Haile, *Jamestown Narratives,* 779.
9. Kupperman, *Captain John Smith,* 239.
10. Ibid., 261, n. 34. The quoted passage is from Smith's *Advertisement for the Unexperienced Planters of New England, or Any Where. Or, the Pathway to Experience to Erect a Plantation* (London, 1631) and reads as follows: "Yet when the foundation is laid, as I have said, and a common-wealth established, then [those who reside] there may better be constrained to labor than [those who remain] here. But *to rectify a common-wealth with debauched people is impossible,* and no wise man would throw himself into such a society, who [has] honest intentions, and knows what he undertakes, for there is no country to pillage as the Romans found: all you expect from thence must be labor."(emphasis added and text modernized to make it more intelligible)
11. Ibid., 17.
12. Haile mentioned them in his reconstruction of the Great Charter of 1618: "Particular (private) plantations must be of contiguous land, and may not exist within five miles of a borough or ten miles of one another—Smith's Hundred, Martin's Hundred, Martin's Brandon, Argall's, Delaware's, Lawne's." Haile, *Jamestown Narratives,* 37. Information about these and other of Virginia's earliest private plantations can be found online at http://en.wikipedia.org/wiki/Category:James_River_plantations.
13. Rubin, *Virginia,* 8.
14. Morgan, *American Slavery,* 90.
15. "And granting by these [ ] unto the said Sir Thomas Gates Sir George Somers Richard Hackluit Edward Maria Wingfield and their associates of the first Colony and unto the said Thomas Hanham, Raleigh Gilbert William Parker, and George Popham and their associates of the said second colony and to every of them from time to time and at all times for ever hereafter power and authority to take and [surprise] by all ways and means whatsoever all and Every person and persons with their Ships Vessels Goods and Other furniture which shall be found trafficking unto any Harbor or harbors Creek or Creeks or places within the Limits and precincts of the said several Colonies and Plantations not being of the same colony until such time as they being of any Realms or Dominions under our obedience shall pay or agree to pay to the hands of the Treasurer of that Colony

within whose limits and precincts they shall so traffic two and a half upon any hundred of anything so by them trafficked bought or sold and being strangers and not subjects under our Obedience until they shall pay five upon every hundred of such wares and commodities as they shall traffic buy or sell within the precincts of the said several Colonies wherein they shall so traffic buy or sell as aforesaid which sums of money or benefit as aforesaid for and during the space of one and twenty years next ensuing the date hereof shall be wholy employed to his benefit and [those] of the said Several Plantations where such traffic shall be made And after the said One and twenty Years Ended the same shall be taken to the use of Us our heirs and successors by such Officer and Minister as by us Our heirs and successors shall be hereunto assigned or appointed And we do further by these presents for us Our Heirs and successors give and grant unto the said Sir Thomas Gates Sir George Summers Richard Hackluit and Edward Maria Wingfield and to their associates of the said first Colony and plantation and to the said Thomas Hanham Raleigh Gilbert William Parker and George Popham and their associates of the said second colony and plantation that they and every of them by their Deputies Ministers and Factors may transport the goods, chattels, armor, munitions and furniture needful to be had by them for their said apparel Defense or otherwise in respect of the said plantations out of our Realm of England and Ireland and all other our Dominions from time to time for and during the time of seven years...." *Charters*, vol. 6, 12–13.

16. *Records*, vol. 3, 122–123.
17. Ibid., 125.
18. Ibid.
19. Hobbes, *Leviathan*, 228–229.
20. "Of systems subordinate, some are political, and some are private. Political (otherwise called bodies politic, and persons in law,) are those, which are made by authority from the sovereign power of the Common-wealth." Ibid., 274.
21. Locke, *Second Treatise,* para. 14, pp. 276–277.
22. Ibid., para. 123, p. 350; para. 124, pp. 350–351.
23. Sir George Yeardley served three terms as a governor of the colony of Virginia: 1616–1617, 1619–1621, and 1626–1627. Yeardley owed his prominence to his association with Sir Thomas Gates, under whom he served during the English campaign in the Netherlands in 1596. Yeardley began his service in the English army as foot soldier and rose

to become Captain of Gates' personal guard. When Sir Thomas Smythe appointed Gates Deputy Governor of the Colony of Virginia in 1609, Gates made Yeardley a member of his staff. Yeardley was with Gates on Admiral George Somers' flagship, the *Sea Venture,* when it wrecked on Bermuda and he assisted Gates in building an escape vessel during the ten months they were stranded on the island. He reached Jamestown the following year in Gates' makeshift craft. Don Jordan and Michael Welsh provided this history of the connection between the men who led the settlement of the Virginia Company's colony in Jamestown: "A few months before the *Trades Increase* [Thomas Smythe's 1200 Indiaman] was launched [in 1609], Smythe took over the direction of the Virginia Company. An immediate and critical decision was made to appoint the right caliber of men to take control of the colony on the ground. Whoever was picked as governor would have autocratic powers and an almost monarchical status. The choice fell on 34-year-old Thomas West, Baron De La Warr. He and Smythe were old comrades. They had fought along side each other in the raid against Cadiz [under Sir Francis Drake in 1587] where both had been commended for bravery, and both had later been caught up in the Essex Rebellion but had survived. They had much in common and no doubt were of a mind on how to revive fortunes in America. Smythe appointed three seasoned fighting men to serve under De La Warr: Sir George Somers who had fought under Sir Walter Raleigh, was made admiral of a new fleet to relieve the colony; Sir Thomas Gates, a veteran of the Netherlands, was appointed Deputy Governor; and Sir Thomas Dale, another veteran of the Dutch War, was made High Marshal." Jordan and Welsh, *White Cargo,* 55–56.

24. *Records,* vol. 3, 122. "Our intent being according to the rules of Justice and good government to a lot unto every one his due yet so as neither to breed disturbance to the right of others nor to interrupt the good form of government intended for the benefit of the people and strength of the colony...." Ibid., 128.

25. Library of Congress, *Colonial Settlement,* "Implementing the Great Charter."

26. Seven of the eleven districts were constituted of grants the company had made to men who were either shareholders or its colonial agents. These precincts included Captain John Martin's Plantation, Smythe's Hundred, Martin's Hundred, Argall's Guiffe, Flowerdieu Hundred, Captain Lawne's Plantation, and Captain Warde's Plantation. Four precincts were not privately owned. These were James City, Charles

City, the City of Henricus, and Kiccowtan. *Records,* vol. 3, 122 ff.

27. Ibid., 197.

28. "Members of the House of Burgesses were the only colonial officials who were elected by popular vote during the entire colonial era. All freemen were eligible to cast ballots in these elections from 1619 to 1670, with the exception of the year 1655, when the franchise was restricted to freeholders (owners of real estate). The following year it was restored to all freemen. Voting requirements were tightened in 1670, and the franchise was limited to freeholders and householders." Dabney, *Virginius,* 42.

29. The company monopolized the colony's commerce with its magazines and "cape merchants."

30. "About the latter end of August, a Dutch man war of the burden of a 160 tunes arrived at Point Comfort, the commander's name Capt Jope, his pilot for the West Indies on Mr Marmaduke an Englishman. They met with the Treasurer in the West Indies, and determined to hold consort ship hetherward, but in their passage lost one the other. He brought not anything but 20 and odd Negroes, which the governor and cape merchant bought for victuals (whereof he was in great need as he pretended) at the best and easiest rate they could." Letter from John Rolfe to Edwin Sandys, Jan 1619/20; *Records,* vol. 3, 243.

31. *Records,* vol. 1, 27.

32. Morgan, *American Slavery,* 117–118.

33. Ibid., 113.

34. *Records,* vol. 1, 480.

35. Ibid., 98.

36. Ibid., 480.

37. "The income which enabled the company to provide for new industries in 1619 and 1620 was derived from the L12.10s paid by each new adventurer for each new share of stock, and from lotteries. Special collections and particular gifts for the advancement of religion and of education in the colony were frequent, and thus the account and management of the college land became important. Before introduction of freedom of trade into the colony, and the dissolution of the magazine on January 12, 1619/20, the company had some profit from that monopoly, but the ease with which returns came from lotteries had doubtless led the company to abolish the monopoly of trade, which had become so difficult to maintain." Ibid., 93.

38. Ibid., 94–95.

39. For an account of this event, see Beverly, *History,* para. 45–48.

40. "[A]fter finding that the company records showed 3570 persons sent to the colony in three years under the Sandys program and that 700 had been already there, for a total of 4270, he [Samuel Wrote] discovered that only 1240 were alive at the time of the massacre. Morgan, *American Slavery*, 101.

41. *Records,* vol. 1, 95–96.

42. Sandys "signified that my Lord Treasurer out of his personal Duty as also the duty of his place bending his thoughts to the advancing of his Majesty's profit and revenue, and yet careful to avoid grieving of his Majesty's subjects and in particular out of his noble affection and well wishing to the plantation, wherein himself was one of the most ancient adventurers, as also of long time a counselor for the same had been pleased of late to make an overture to him for contracting with the two companies of Virginia and Somer Islands for the sole importation of tobacco into England, as also into the realms of Ireland: the grant whereof having in these two former years been managed by other contractors to the discontent and perhaps detriment of the said plantations, they might now have the sole managing of all that commodity with reservation of a valuable rent to his Majesty which he thought might redound to the great benefit of the plantations." Ibid., vol. 2, 36.

43. Ibid., 81.

44. Ibid.

45. Ibid., 85.

46. Ibid.

47. Morgan, *American Slavery,* 122.

48. *Records,* vol. 1.

49. Beverly, *History,* para. 52, p. 56.

50. *Records,* vol. 3, 502–503.

51. Washburn, *Virginia under Charles I,* 4–5.

52. Ibid., 5.

53. Ibid., 8.

54. Morgan, *American Slavery*, 141.

55. Ibid., 144.

56. Beverly, *History,* para. 54, pp. 57–58.

57. Washburn, *Virginia under Charles I,* 9.

58. Ibid., 20.

59. Beverly, *History,* para. 56–57, pp. 58–59.

60. Ibid., para. 58, pp. 59–60.

61. Ibid., para. 59, p. 60.

62. Billings, *The Papers.*
63. *Journal of the House of Burgesses,* 76.
64. That the burgesses were aware of this is confirmed in the record of the proceedings of the Grand Assembly of 5 April 1647: "Now for as much as rumors & reports are raised and spread abroad, that by a late ordinance of the Parliament of England, all strangers are prohibited trade with any of the English plantations, which we conceive to be the inventions of some English merchants on purpose to affright & expel the Dutch, and make way for themselves to monopolize not only our labors and fortunes, but even our persons, which we may with so much sense of smart deliver, in that with the confidence of truth we may aver, that the monopolies, contracts & projects of our commodity designed upon & against us by the English merchants for false end, & to our ruin have cost us more in charges of assemblies, then would have sufficiently fortified the country with the advantage of many a profitable nursery for manufactures." The assembly concluded on this defiant note: "In order whereupon, we do again invite the Dutch Nation, & again publish & declare all freedom & liberty to them to trade within the colony. And do oblige ourselves & the whole colony to defend them with our uttermost power & ability, in the peaceable fruition thereof either by reparation from the estates of those who shall offer them any violence or cause them any disturbance otherwise & shall proceed against them as oppugners of our undoubted rights & privileges." Ibid., 74.
65. Ibid., 77–78.
66. Beverly, *History,* para. 65, p. 63.
67. "The plantation of Virginia and all the inhabitants thereof" agreed to remain "in due obedience and subjection to the common wealth of England, according to the laws there established." The Grand Assembly was then recommissioned to "convene and transact the affairs of Virginia, wherein nothing is to be acted or done contrary to the government of the common wealth of England and the laws there established." The colony was to retain its "ancient bounds and limits granted by the charters of the former Kings. All the patents of land granted under the colony seal" were to remain "in their full force and strength." The practice of granting a fifty-acre headright "for every person transported in the colony" was to continue. The colony was to have "free trade as the people of Virginia do enjoy to all places and with all nations according to the laws of that common wealth." No taxes were to be imposed on the colony "without

consent of the Grand Assembly." Parishioners could use their old Book of Common Prayer for another year. The colonial quitrents that the king had granted to Parliament were to hold for seven years. "The present Governor, that is Sir William Berkeley and the Council shall have leave to sell and dispose of their estates, and to transport themselves whether they please. That all persons that are now in the colony of what quality or condition soever that have served the King here or in England shall be free from all dangers, punishment or mulkt whatsoever...." *Journal of the House of Burgesses*, 79–81.

68. Ibid., 42.

69. Billings, "Sir William Berkeley."

70. In its meeting on 24 March 1657, for example, the Assembly resolved: "Whereas Major William Lewis preferred a petition to the house therein requesting that the commission might be granted unto them to discover the Mountains & Westward ports of the Country & to endeavor the finding out of any Commodities that might probably then to the benefit of this Country. It is ordered for the encouragement to them & others that shall be of the like public and generous spirits that a commission shall be granted them to authorize their undertaking and all such gentlemen as shall voluntarily accompany them in the said discovery." Billings, *The Papers*, 106.

71. Ibid., 107.

72. "This Grand Assembly taking into their consideration the inequality of raising taxes per poll, And the small encouragement given to any public endeavors by reason of the inconsiderable value of levy tobacco, It is therefore ordered that two shillings per hundred be laid upon every hundred of tobacco exported out of this country, out of which money to be so raised six hundred pounds sterling to be paid to the honorable Samuel Mathews, Esquire, Governor." Ibid., 108.

73. Ibid.

74. Ibid., 111.

75. Washburn, *Virginia under Charles I.*

76. Billings, *The Papers*, 111.

77. Churchill reported: "[O]f the Commons there remained nothing but the few survivors contemptuously named the Rump.... It was the surviving embodiment of the Parliamentary cause. Its members felt that the country would need their guidance for many a long year." He described the demise of their government in these words: "The Rump prospered only so long as their Lord General [Cromwell] was at the wars. When he returned victorious he was struck by their unpopular-

ity. He was also shocked by their unrepresentative character. Above all, he observed that the Army, hitherto occupied about God's business in other directions, looked sourly on their civilian masters and paymasters. He labored to mediate between the shrunken Parliament and its gigantic sword, but even he could not withhold his criticism. He loathed the war against the Protestant Dutch. He deprecated Licensing Acts and Treason Acts, which overrode customary liberties. Finally he convinced himself of the 'pride, ambition, and self-seeking' of the remaining Members of Parliament. He foresaw sad dangers should they succeed in what he now feared was their design of perpetuating their rule. He looked upon them with the same disparaging glance as Napoleon, returned from Egypt, cast upon the Directory. The oligarchs, dwelling under the impression that Parliamentary supremacy had been for ever established by the execution of the King, and heedless of their tottering foundations, remained obdurate. The Lord General's outlook was clear and his language plain. 'These men,' Oliver said, 'will never leave till the Army pull them down by the ears." He accordingly went to the House on April 20, 1653, accompanied by thirty musketeers. He took his seat and for a time listened to the debate. Then rising in his place, he made a speech which grew in anger as it proceeded. 'Come, come,' he concluded, 'I will put an end to your prating. You are no Parliament.' He called in his musketeers to clear the House and lock the doors. While the indignant politicians, most of whom were men of force and fire, were being hustled into the street the General's eye fell on the Mace, symbol of the Speaker's authority. 'What shall I do with this bauble?' he asked. 'Take it away!'... One man's will now ruled. One puzzled, self-questioning, but explosive spirit became for a spell the guardian of the slowly gathered work of ages...." Churchill, *A History*, 301–302.

78. Ibid., 195.
79. Cited by Fraser, *Royal Charles*, 195.
80. Rubin, *Virginia*, 19.
81. "Crops of half a million had ended the boom prices of the 1620s. By 1663 the official count of tobacco reaching the port of London alone was over seven million pounds; in 1669, nine million pounds; in 1672, ten and half million pounds; and the planter had to sell for half or less what he had generally got in the 1640s and 1650s." Morgan, *American Slavery*, 185.
82. According to Morgan, "tobacco duties from Virginia and Maryland accounted for perhaps 25 percent of England's customs revenue

and 5 percent of the government's total income in the 1660s." Ibid., 193.

83. The men who received the Northern Neck grant all appear to have been those who aided him in his flight from England after his defeat at the Battle of Worcester in 1651. *Ralph, Lord Hoptson* had led the royalist armies in the west prior to Charles' flight; *John, Lord Berkeley* (later Baron of Stratton) was one of Lord Hoptson's commanders. *Henry, Lord Jermyn* (later Baron of St. Edmundsbury and then Earl of St Albans) was confidante and secretary to Charles' mother, Queen Henrietta Maria. Having served as governor of the Island of Jersey in 1644, he conducted Prince Charles from there to Paris in 1647. *John, Lord Culpeper* (1st Baron of Thoresway 1600–1660) was among the party that accompanied Charles in this final phase of his journey into exile. *Sir William Morton, Sir Dudley Wyatt,* and *Thomas Culpeper, Esq.* (cousin-german of Lord John) had served the king during the war and were apparently members of the prince's retinue on this journey.

84. Hoptson, Morton, Wyatt, and Thomas Culpeper all died prior to 1660.

85. Osgood, *The American Colonies,* 147.

86. Ibid., 149.

87. The Carteret family held estates on the island of Jersey, and Lord George was in Charles' company while he tarried there on his way to France in 1647. James himself is listed as the governor from 1645 to 1650.

88. Wertenbaker, *Bacon's Rebellion,* 2.

89. Morton, *Colonial Virginia,* 207–208.

90. Edmund Morgan reported, "the Northern Neck had grown in population more rapidly than any other part of Virginia in the years since 1652. The inhabitants had risen from about 1,300, or about 9 percent of Virginia's population in 1653, to perhaps 6,000, or about 19 percent in 1674." Morgan, *American Slavery,* 244–245.

91. Culpeper sought to possess a quitrent revenue that Virginia's Treasurer, Sir Henry Norwood, had collected *in absentia* since 1661. Sir Henry was another loyalist of the civil war era whom the king preferred with this and other lucrative appointments.

92. Morton, *Colonial Virginia,* 208.

93. Ibid., 209–210.

94. Beverly, *History,* para. 92, p. 74.

95. Ibid., para. 93, pp. 75–76.

96. Morton, *Colonial Virginia*, 210.
97. Harrison, *The Proprietors*; http://www.gen.culpeper.com/historical/
    nneck/5a-leeds.htm#Catherine.
98. Hendrick, *The Lees of Virginia*, 45.
99. Beverly, *History*, para. 127, p. 94.
100. Hendrick, *The Lees of Virginia*, 45.
101. Ibid., 31.
102. Peterson, *Writings*, 262.
103. *Records*, vol. 1.
104. Much of the information in this chapter comes from Dunstan, "Co-
    lonial Alexandria." A copy of this publication was graciously pro-
    vided by Michael Miller, historian of the City of Alexandria.
105. Sutton, *Revolution to Succession*, 1.
106. Ibid., 72.
107. Peterson, *Writings*, 106.
108. Ibid., 110.
109. *The Journal of the Continental Congress* was kept by Charles Thomson
    who held the post of Secretary of the Congress. One finds in Thom-
    son's records that the Congress never formally approved the colonial
    "Bill of Rights" that John Adams drafted and vigorously promoted.
    Since the Congress did not approve this document, it could not have
    ratified a "declaration" that contained it. A "Declaration of Rights
    and Grievances" nevertheless appears in the records as printed by
    Thomson. How could this be? Adams probably manufactured the
    document between 22 October and 26 October while serving as a
    committee of one to prepare the records of the Congress for publi-
    cation. In the course of his midnight editing, Adams connected his
    unratified draft for a colonial bill of rights with General John Sul-
    livan's report on colonial grievances. Thomson cleverly inserted this
    Declaration of Rights and Grievances into his entry for the proceed-
    ings of the Congress on 14 October, which was the day the Congress
    had considered the two sets of resolutions. The cooperative effort of
    these two patriots allowed the "radical party" to escape a humiliat-
    ing political setback while at the same time preempting a potentially
    disruptive conservative reaction. Accomplishing all this was simpler
    than it might otherwise have been because most of the delegates had
    departed from Philadelphia before Thomson perpetrated his ruse.
    Few of the Congress' delegates probably read the 14 October entry
    before the hot war began six months later. When it did, attitudes
    among conservatives changed and Thomson's sleight of hand be-

came a dead issue. Thomson's maneuver therefore succeeded and Adams' bill of rights became a living document in America's history. *The Declaration of Rights and Grievances* is found in the *Journal of the Library of Congress*, 63–73.

Bibliography

Andrews, Charles McLean. *The Colonial Period of American History*. New Haven: Yale University Press, 1934.

————. *Colonial Self Government 1652–1689*. New York: Harper Brothers, 1904.

Beer, George Davis. *The Old Colonial System 1660–1754*. New York: Mac-Millan, 1912.

Beverly, Robert. *The History and Present State of Virginia*. Charlottesville: University Press of Virginia, 1947.

Billings, Warren M., ed. *The Papers of Sir William Berkeley 1605-1677*. Richmond, VA: Library of Virginia, 2007. http://www.uno.edu/~history/berkeley.htm.

————. "Sir William Berkeley." *Virtual Jamestown, Jamestown Interpretive Essays*. http://www.virtualjamestown.org/essays/billings_essay.html.

————. *Sir William Berkeley and the Forging of Colonial Virginia*. Baton Rouge: Louisiana State University Press, 1965.

Bond, Beverly W. *The Quitrent System in the American Colonies*. New Haven: Yale University Press, 1919.

Bruce, Philip A. *Institutional History of Virginia*. New York: P. G. Putnam, 1910.

Charters of the Virginia Company of London; Laws, Abstracts of Rolls in the Office of State. Vol. 6. *Virginia Manuscripts, 1607–1737*. "Thomas Jefferson Papers Series 8." Washington, DC: Library of Congress.

Churchill, Winston. *A History of the English Speaking Peoples*. Vol. 2. New York: Dodd, Mead, & Company, 1956.

Dabney, Virginius. *Virginia, The New Dominion*. Charlottesville: University Press of Virginia, 1971.

Dunstan, Effie Crittenden. "Colonial Alexandria 1749–1776: The Governmental Power Structure," in *A Composite History of Alexandria*. Alexandria, VA: Alexandria Bicentennial Commission, 1975.

Fiske, John. *Historical Writings: Vol. 4, Old Virginia and Her Neighbors.* Standard Library Edition. Cambridge, MA: Riverside Press, 1902.

Fraser, Antonia. *Royal Charles - Charles II and the Restoration.* New York: Dell Publishing, Delta Book, 1979.

Great Britain. Board of Trade. *Journal of the Commissioners for Trade and Plantations.* London: Public Record Office, 1938.

Great Britain. Public Record Office. *Calendar of State Papers: Colonial Series, America and West Indies, 1574.* By Sir John William Fortescue. London, 1928.

Haile, Edward Wright, ed. *Jamestown Narratives: Eyewitness Accounts of the Virginia Colony (The First Decade: 1606-1617)* Champlain, VA: RoundHouse, 1998.

Hamor, Ralphe. *A True Discourse on the Present Estate of Virginia, and the Successe of the Affaires There until the 18 of June 1614.* The Capital and the Bay: Narratives of Washington and the Chesapeake Bay Region, ca. 1600-1925. Washington, DC: Library of Congress. Published by Albany J. Munsell, 1860. Call Number: F229.H19. Digital ID: lhbcb 02778.

Harrison, Fairfax. *The Proprietors of the Northern Neck: Chapters of Culpeper Genealogy.* N.p.: n.p.,1926; *Culpeper Connection! The Culpeper Family History Site.* http://www.gen.culpeper.com/historical/nneck/5a-leeds.htm.

———. *Virginia Land Grants: A Study of Conveyancing in Relation to Colonial Politics.* Westminster, MD: Heritage Books reprint, 2007.

Hendrick, Burton. *The Lees of Virginia: Biography of a Family.* Boston: Little Brown, 1935.

Hobbes, Thomas. *Leviathan.* New York: Penguin Classics, 1985.

Isaac, Rhys. *The Transformation of Virginia, 1740–1790.* Chapel Hill: Omohundro Institute of Early American History and Culture, University of North Carolina Press, 1999.

Jordan, Don, and Michael Welsh. *White Cargo: The Forgotten History of Britain's White Slaves in America.* New York: New York University Press, 2008.

Journal of the House of Burgesses of Virginia 1619–1658/9. Edited by H. R. McIlwaine, Richmond, VA: n.p., 1915.

Journal of the Continental Congress. "The Declaration of Rights and Grievances" **Washington, DC: Government Printing Office, 1904.**

Kammen, Michael. *Deputyes and Libertyes: The Origins of Representative Government in Colonial America.* New York: Alfred A. Knopf, 1969.

Kupperman, Karen Ordahl, ed., *Captain John Smith: A Select Edition of His Writings.* Chapel Hill, NC: University of North Carolina Press, 1988.

Library of Congress. *Colonial Settlement, 1600s–1763.* "Implementing the Great Charter in Virginia, 1619." http://www.loc.gov/teachers/classroommaterials/presentationsandactivities/presentations/timeline/colonial/virginia/charter.html.

Locke, John. *Second Treatise of Government.* Edited by Peter Laslett. Cambridge, England: Cambridge University Press, Paperback edition, 1991.

Morgan, Edmund. *American Slavery - American Freedom.* New York: W. W. Norton, 1975.

Morton, Richard L. *Colonial Virginia,* Vol. 1. Chapel Hill, NC: University of North Carolina Press, 1960.

Osgood, Herbert L. *The American Colonies in the Seventeenth Century.* Vol. 3. New York: Columbia University Press, 1904-1907.

Parkinson, Andrew. "Sir Edwin Sandys." *Northbourne Sources,* biographical information. http://freespace.virgin.net/andrew.parkinson4/san_intr.html.

Peterson, Merrill, ed. *The Writings of Thomas Jefferson.* New York: Library of America, 1984.

The Records of the Virginia Company of London. Vols. 1-4. Bowie, MD: Heritage Books, 1999. Edited by Susan Myra Kingsbury.

The Records of the Virginia Company, 1606-1627. Vol. 3. "Thomas Jefferson Papers Series 8." *Virginia Manuscripts, 1607-1737.* Washington, DC: Library of Congress. Miscellaneous Records.

Robinson, W. Stitt. *Mother Earth Land Grants in Virginia 1607–1699.* Williamsburg, VA: Virginia 350th Anniversary Celebration Corporation, 1957.

Rubin, Louis. *Virginia, A History.* New York: W. W. Norton, 1984.

Sutton, Robert P. *Revolution to Succession.* Charlottesville, VA: University Press of Virginia, 1989.

Thorpe, Francis Newton, ed. *The Federal and State Constitutions Colonial Charters, and Other Organic Laws of the States, Territories, and Colonies Now or Heretofore Forming the United States of America.* Compiled and edited under the Act of Congress of June 30, 1906. Washington, DC: Government Printing Office, 1909.

Washburn, Wilcomb. *Virginia under Charles I and Cromwell, 1625-1660.* Williamsburg, VA: Virginia 350th Anniversary Celebration Corporation, 1957.

Wertenbaker, Thomas J. *Bacon's Rebellion, 1676.* Williamsburg, VA: Virginia 350th Anniversary Celebration Corporation, 1957.

Wright, Louis. *The Library of Richard Lee, the Scholar: Richard Lee II, a Belated Elizabethan in Virginia.* Published in the October 1938 issue of

The Huntington Library Quarterly 2 (October 1938): 1–35. http://www. huntington.org/huntingtonlibrary_03.aspx?id=2988&terms=huntingt on+library+quarterly.

Index

Some key terms are italicized and underlined in the index.
Page numbers of illustrations appear in bold.

About the Author

J AMES THOMPSON holds undergraduate and graduate degrees
in Philosophy from the University of Virginia. His interest in
American history developed as a graduate student living on the
Shadwell, Virginia farm of Thomas Jefferson's daughter, Martha
Jefferson Randolph. James completed the research for *The Birth of
Virginia's Aristocracy* as a Batten Fellow at the International Center
for Jefferson Studies at Monticello in 2005.